WRITEFUL

Gary Hoffman
Professor of English and Art

VERVE PRESS

Copyright © 1986 by Gary Hoffman

Printed in the United States of America

ISBN 0-937363-00-6
Library of Congress Catalogue Card Number: 85-52460
Published by Verve Press, P.O. Box 1997, Huntington Beach, California, 92647.

All rights reserved. No part of this book may be reproduced or transmitted in any form or by any means, electronic or mechanical, including photocopying, recording or by any information storage and retrieval system without written permission from the publisher, except for brief quotations embodied in critical articles and reviews. For information, write Verve Press, P.O. Box 1997, Huntington Beach, California, 92647.

First Printing 1986
Typesetting: Darby's Typography, Inc.
Printing: KNI
Cover design: Gary Hoffman

Grateful acknowledgment is made for permission to use excerpts from the following in order of appearance:

"Hound Dog," by Jerry Leiber and Mike Stoller. Copyright © 1956 by Elvis Presley Music, Inc. and Lion Publishing Co., Inc. Copyright renewed, assigned to Gladys Music (administered by Chappell & Co., Inc.; Intersong Music, Publisher) MCA Music, a division of MCA, Inc. International copyright secured, all rights reserved. Reprinted with permission of Chappell/Intersong.
House Made of Dawn by N. Scott Momaday, Copyright © 1968 by N. Scott Nomaday. Reprinted with permission of Harper & Row.
"God Is Dead In Georgia," Excerpts from the *Diaries of the Late God,* by Anthony Towne. Printed in *motive* magazine, copyright © 1966 by the General Board of Higher Education and Ministry of the United Methodist Church, reprinted by permission of the board's office of interpretation.
"Thirteen Ways of Looking at a Blackbird," *The Collected Poems of Wallace Stevens,* copyright © 1954 by Wallace Stevens, reprinted by permission of Alfred A. Knopf, Inc.
"New York Style," in *New York,* compiled by Peter Blauner, copyright © 1985 by News Group Publications, Inc., reprinted by permission of *New York* magazine.
"Last Night I Drove a Car," *Gasoline,* copyright © by Gregory Corso 1955, reprinted by permission of City Lights Books.
Letter to His Father by Franz Kafka, trans. Ernst Kaiser and Eithne Wilkins, copyright © 1953, 1954, 1966 by Schocken Books Inc., reprinted by permission of Schocken Books Inc.
Other references are listed under "Notes" in the back of this book and are used in accordance with Section 107 of the United States Copyright Act.

ABOUT THE AUTHOR

Gary Hoffman was born in El Paso, Texas and later moved to California where he attended Pasadena High School. He studied architecture at U.C. Berkeley, then transferred to U.C.L.A., changed his major to English and art, and received his B.A. in 1969. After obtaining his M.A. in English at U.C.L.A., he started working on a Ph.D. in English at U.S.C. where he also taught freshman composition. In 1971 he became a full-time faculty member in the English department at Orange Coast College in Costa Mesa, California, where he has been teaching writing for over fifteen years. He is also an adjunct member of the art department and has taught design and cartooning. Gary's interests include international cinema, landscape design, and native and folk art. His wife, Deena, teaches high school English. They have two children, Casey and Jesse.

CONTENTS

About the Author

Preface

Acknowledgments

Disclaimer

PART I FULL-BRAIN STYLE

1. STARTING WITH FIRE 11
   Introduction to Full-Brain Style

2. SMOOTHING THE FLOW 14
   Ways to speed pace and hold on
       to long thoughts
   Railroad Ramble 15
   Telescoping Sentences 20

3. GIVING PAUSE 25
   Ways to slow pace and give punch
       to quick thoughts
   The Very Short Sentence 26
   Traditional Hieroglyphics 29
   Melted-Together Words 32
   Innocent Language 35

4. FINE-TUNING REALITY 40
   Ways to spark interest in truth with metaphor
   Slang Hang 43
   Body Parts 46
   Line Ups 48
   Mix Masters 48

5. MAKING FACES 56
   Ways to avoid insincerity and intimidation
   Facial Packs 57
   War Paint 61
   Metal Mask 64

CONTENTS continued

PART II   FULL-BLOODED STRATEGY

1. PUTTING TOGETHER HUMPTY-DUMPTY ... 71
   Introduction to Full-Blooded Strategy

2. RAISING THE DEAD 74
   Resurrecting past ideas

3. SPLITTING THE SECOND 77
   Detailing momentary realities

4. MOCKING WITH MASS MEDIA 81
   Deflating media or mentalities

5. ANIMAL TALK 85
   Capturing zoological details

6. NICE GIANTS 90
   Sketching positive achievements

7. UGLY GIANTS 94
   Undercutting products or mentalities

8. THIRTEEN WAYS OF LOOKING
   AT A BLACKBIRD 99
   Capturing complex subjects

9. SLICED PIE 104
   Simplifying complex subjects

10. STRIP TEASE 111
    Narrowing towards truth and revelation

11. FLASHBACK 117
    Intensifying reflection

12. DOUBLE EXPOSURES 123
    Revealing double-layered realities

13. DEVIL'S ADVICE 129
    Spoiling self-righteous arguments

14. TALKING WORDS 135
    Defining abstract concepts

15. BLOOD FLOW 140
    Revealing omnipresent forces

CONTENTS continued

PART II FULL-BLOODED STRATEGY continued

16 DOORS 146
    Building ideas from openings

17 SQUEEZE PLAY 154
    Asking for love

18 FINGER POINT 159
    Amplifying messages

19 SINCERELY YOURS 165
    Revealing truth in letters

20 MASKS 170
    Eyeing new realities

21 NAY, IT IS. I KNOW NOT 'SEEMS.' 175
    Revealing implicit truths

22 REAL MAGIC 181
    Snagging dreamy truths

23 FRAME UPS 187
    Explaining with dialogue

24 DUST IN THE LIBRARY 193
    Avoiding dead research papers

25 BILLY FAULKNER 199
    Inventing full-blooded strategy

NOTES 203

PREFACE

WRITEFUL is for all who believe writing can be a challenging yet creative experience, that from the beginning, learning to write need not be a dry, scaly pursuit resulting in dead writing. WRITEFUL is also for those who believe talking about what makes good writing should be an interesting, sometimes entertaining, endeavor, and not simply a beast of instructional burden.

Being both a teacher and continuing student of writing, and still remembering myself as a beginning student of writing, I now realize a crucial point about learning to write. Mature or intelligent beginning writers crave learning about complex writing principles over simplistic ones so long as that complexity is demystified and made intriguing. When this happens, those students' interests overlap the interests of advanced writers. Therefore, unlike most books on writing, WRITEFUL does not assume a narrowly defined audience, but addresses many groups at once, including advanced high school writers, college freshmen, self-taught writers, teachers, and professional writers.

One important key to designing a book that demystifies the complexity of good writing is to realize that writing involves more than left-brain, linear, rational thinking. This book assumes that people enjoy improving their writing when explanations and work outs also appeal to the right brain's craving for visual imagery, what "sounds right," or what can be discovered through play. This side of thinking makes writing pliable, a clay that can be shaped and controlled. It keeps the rational mind from turning writing into a stony-walled labyrinth that blocks full-blooded writing. When a writing book stimulates both a writer's reason and imagination, that writer is more fully engaged and more resourceful than conventional teaching permits.

Conventional, learning-to-write books claim to offer a more successful way to write, but most are snatchers. They cannibalize each other, grinding out old concepts with familiar models, exercises, and assignments. Also many of these books make distinctions between advanced writers and remedial writers. As mentioned above, WRITEFUL does not make this assumption, but helps all writers. However, advanced writers might have more sophisticated or mature responses to the work outs in this book than remedial students. This book does assume that a student has an innate sentence sense: the student can hear whether a sentence is complete when it is read aloud, even if he or she cannot see that it is.

Part I of this book, FULL-BRAIN STYLE, gives writers principles for writing sentences that are a distillation of traditional grammars. Principles are structures that appeal to rational thinking, but the synthesized principles of FULL-BRAIN STYLE appeal to a person's desire to have only a few imperative rules before plunging into self-discovery, an advantage enjoyed for years by students in studio art classes. In FULL-BRAIN STYLE, these rules are tools that encourage interesting, varied sentences with vivid diction. The rules explain how to replace safe, monotonous, bland writing.

Part II of this book, FULL-BLOODED STRATEGY, sets up writing pursuits that are applicable to a very wide range of situations demanding good writing. These pursuits have enough examples to clarify the writing tasks without relying on complete essays that sometimes are distracting, delaying written action. The strategies in Part II are full-blooded: they encourage structures and points of view that are inventive and allow for enthusiasm and passion.

Gary Hoffman 1985

ACKNOWLEDGMENTS

Books are the product of an author's circumstances and of the people with whom an author has been intimate. This book could not have been written without the appreciation of teaching problems and editorial skills of my wife, Deena Hoffman. Also this book would not exist if not for the encouragement and hundreds of creative dialogues with my best friend and colleague for over fifteen years, Gary Freeman.

This book is also a direct result of my experience with many of the students at Orange Coast College who have taken my writing classes. I decided to write this book primarily because of those students' delight and success with the instructional spirit and lively materials that now enliven this book.

The Orange Coast College English department of 1971-1979 is also responsible for this book. It is hard to imagine an English department more democratic and devoid of take-ourselves-seriously syndrome, as that particular one. In those vital years, the atmosphere they created fueled this book's booster stage.

The spirit of this book can be traced to my parents. My mother and stepfather, Professors Roberta and Pete Markman, encouraged me to go into teaching and to assume that creativity was possible within the constraints of academia. From my father, Al Hoffman, I learned to delight in the nuances of different verbal styles and story telling. My brother, Professor Glenn Hoffman, has always helped keep that delight alive.

Very special thanks to Judy Russo, Marie Clifford and Pete for their thoughtful editorial consultations. I also thank Phil Miller of Prentice-Hall, Nancy Perry of St. Martin's Press, Steve Pensinger of Random House, Betsy Perry of John Wiley & Sons, Bill McLane of Harcourt Brace Jovanovich, Ann Smith of Scott, Foresman, and Paul Smith of D.C. Heath for their encouragement and helpful commentary.

DISCLAIMER

Writing is a complex matter and no single book on the subject can cover everything about how to write or what makes for good writing. The purpose of this book is to complement, amplify, and supplement other books on writing. WRITEFUL is not the final word of the gods.

Writing is an enjoyable, creative, and challenging endeavor. Often it is a passionate or moral act. As such, writing sometimes can be risky. This text encourages writers to take risks but the appropriateness of those risks is determined by one's intimate knowledge of the varying nuances that change from situation to situation at one's place of learning, business, and personal life. Only the writer who uses this book can judge those situations and not the author or publisher of this book. Also, any of the advice in this text can be abused, misused, or followed without complete understanding. The author and publisher of this text will not be responsible for such misuse. WRITEFUL does not replace the wisdom of the gods.

One of the purposes of this book is to motivate good writing and to provide new ways of thinking about writing. Most readers of this book will improve their writing skills and understanding of writing. But learning to write well takes much practice, maturity, and time. This text does not pretend to teach one how to write overnight. WRITEFUL is not the gods' ambrosia.

Every effort has been made to make this book complete and as accurate as possible. However, there may be mistakes both typographical and in content. The purpose of this book is to educate and entertain. The author and Verve Press shall have neither liability nor responsibility to any person or entity with respect to any loss or damage caused or alleged to be caused directly or indirectly by the information or advice contained in this book.

PART I
FULL-BRAIN STYLE

1
STARTING WITH FIRE
Introduction to Full-Brain Style

Passion is the most important force in good writing. Excitement and sincere concern for the subject matter lead more quickly to clarity, concreteness, and inventiveness than studying rhetorical devices or grammatical rules. But sometimes even the most passionate and most noble thoughts and feelings can dissolve when they hit paper; therefore, knowing a few full-brain principles can help give writing shape and durability. Full-Brain Style is an attempt to boil down traditional rules, simplify them, and melt them into concepts that are accessible to the playful, creative part of the mind.

Full-Brain Style also assumes that good writing has to start with the smallest parts of writing. Word for word, sentence for sentence, writing must be thoughtful, fun to do, and make a difference. In some ways, sentences and individual words make more difference to a piece of writing than overall organization and overall idea. Often, when we read magazine articles, newspaper columns, short stories, letters, or memos, our memories pin the overall idea or thesis onto one or two well put sentences, and crumble away the skeletal structure of the work we have just read.

Therefore it is dangerous to be strongly focused on the notion that organization is the final resting place for good writing. This can distract from the importance of words and sentences; written vitality can fade, leaving the well-organized paper a hollow shell. Vitality also fades when writers believe that clipping the wings of their words and straight-jacketing their sentences makes writing more "objective." The best writers in all fields, including scientific ones, know that to write accurately, to close in on reality, one in fact cannot write neutered prose. They know words must be shaped and fired.

Full-Brain Style is an attempt to define a grammar that everyone can use for all kinds of writings, that makes writing more exacting, and also gives writing more vitality. It is an attempt to make the smaller parts of writing more fun to work with.

There are four abilities a good writer must possess to shape the smaller, crucial elements of a written piece. "Smoothing the Flow" is the first one. A good writer must be able to feel comfortable writing long, loose sentences that speed with the pace of natural speech. These sentences are crucial in pulling together small ideas or details, creating important connections for the reader. "Smoothing the Flow" deals with some ways to hold onto these connections, giving them shape and at the same time, overriding any of the clipped stiffness that occurs in insecure writing.

"Giving Pause" counter-balances "Smoothing the Flow," slowing writing down in order to bring focus or attention to an item that otherwise might be swirled away in a flow of prose. Good writers must be able to stop or interrupt the flow at key intervals in order to shock, to give punch, or to emphasize something before allowing the reader to continue on. "Giving Pause" offers some intriguing and effective ways to do this.

"Fine-tuning Reality" adds exactness and spark to flow and pause. The most important way to fine-tune is with metaphor. Metaphor is a lively way to make anything that is complicated simpler to understand, or to return vitality to anything that has lost its uniqueness. Many student writers fail to give metaphor high priority because they associate it with cuteness or decoration. Good metaphors have nothing to do with these; in fact, metaphor is essential to all modes of writing: personal, fictional, scientific, and business.

The fourth and last principle discussed in Part I, "Making Faces," has more to do with what not to do than with what to do. Good writing must be sincere, and the healthy writer learns to avoid euphemism, intimidation, and pretension. These tendencies to inflate reality break out when writers really have nothing to say or do not care about what they are saying. With the insecure person, this results in grammatical messes and embarrassing prose, and with professionals, the results are slick versions of insincerity or outright lies. "Making Faces" presents some playful ways to avoid this kind of writing.

2
SMOOTHING THE FLOW
Ways to speed pace and hold on to long thoughts

Before we get to pre-school we know how to say "He throws the ball," and by the time we get out of first grade we can write, maybe with misspellings, "He throws the ball." But by first grade we can say a lot more than we can write, such as "Bill, the guy who is always getting me in trouble and never listens to the teacher, but she always says 'He's trying,' and John, the guy who fed the rat to Kurt, the python at school, both got sick and started throwing up all over the floor, the desks, and Mr. Skumawitz, the new principal everyone calls Skoomie." We can say long sentences, but sometimes, even as adults, we are afraid to write a long sentence like this one.

FULL-BRAIN STYLE

Good writers never kill a good long sentence. They are not afraid to write one because they never worry about how long a sentence will turn out to be or how it will look on paper. If it sounds right when they read it out loud, they are happy. They also know long sentences are necessary and good writers care about making them work. For instance, there are many characters, actions, and subthoughts in the sentence above about John and Bill, but they belong together and naturally flow together to create a reality that is as exciting and as fraught with sideshows as the actual situation described really was. By using a length that smooths reality's flow, the sentence has captured intertwined experiences, which together had created an elongated, prolonged reality.

Following are two methods that smooth the flow: railroad-ramble and telescoping sentences. These are not the only two ways to create sentences that smooth the flow, but they are two useful ones. Once you are able to use them and combine them, you will gain a confidence in writing that allows other natural, long sentences to develop, and these structures almost unconsciously become part of the writer's style.

RAILROAD-RAMBLE

To do railroad-ramble, one takes a simple sentence like "Bill chewed a red apple," and pictures the different parts of the sentence to be on railroad freight cars. Then one simply imagines that each car can have more of the same material snapped onto the top of their loads with commas.

For instance, one may consider the subject of the apple sentence above, Bill, as a railroad car, and examine whether others are eating the apple as well. Snap them onto the "subject" car. "Bill, my aunt Tina, farmer Olson, and all their cronies, chewed a red apple." Next consider the verb or action "car" in the sentence train. Did the subjects only eat the apple or did they do other things to it? A thesaurus and close observation of reality are both helpful in making these considerations. "Bill, my aunt Tina, farmer Olson, and all their cronies, chopped, chewed, and pulverized the red apple."

The object acted upon, "the apple," and the word that describes it, "red," also can be thought of as riding on train cars onto which more of the same material can be snapped. Were just apples worked on, or other foods? What about the apples, were they just red? The final reality train might end up something like this: "Bill, my aunt Tina, farmer Olson, and all their cronies, chopped, chewed, and utterly pulverized the red, hard, juicy, candied apple and the mud-brown, crumbling cookies, scatter-shot with chocolate chips." Snapping on a detail as the train takes off, as with "scatter-shot with chocolate chips," often works out well.

Phrases attached to main sentences can also be viewed as riding on railroad freight cars. For instance, if the first sentence read "While opening the door, Bill chewed a red apple," it might eventually read "While opening the door, tip-toeing across the threshold, and throwing themselves into the hay, Bill, my aunt Tina, farmer Olson, and all their cronies, polished, chopped, chewed, and utterly pulverized the red, hard, juicy, candied apple, and the mudbrown, crumbling cookies, scatter-shot with chocolate chips."

And like the American folk word-game, "The House That Jack Built," the fun does not stop yet. Sentence trains can be switched onto a second track that has its own existing train. If the two are related closely enough in idea, they can be hooked together with connecting words such as "and," "but," "therefore," "or," "besides," "because," and many others, including the semi-colon (;) that can be used with, or replace, some of these connectors. (See chapter 2 for use of the semi-colon and colon.) Connecting different sentence trains, one could build the following: "While opening the door, tip-toeing across the threshold, and throwing themselves onto the hay, Bill, my aunt Tina, farmer Olson, and all their cronies, chopped, chewed, and utterly pulverized the red, hard, juicy, candied apple, and the mudbrown, crumbling cookies, scatter-shot with chocolate chips, but this bizarre, fabricated event is not worth repeating, even if it makes for a cute, telling, or graphic example of a point that could result in my writing a sentence that goes on for a page but says absolutely nothing of any consequence."

FULL-BRAIN STYLE

WORK OUT
After looking over the following examples, write ten railroad-ramble sentences about your past and present life. They should all be several lines long and numbered; do not worry about putting them into an essay. As with the sample sentences, some cars on your trains should be stacked high with weighty material, other cars may be left empty, and sometimes you may connect trains to other trains.

SAMPLES
Set out before it gets hot, and when you are going, walk nicely and quietly and do not run off the path, or you may fall and break the bottle, and then your grandmother will get nothing; and when you go into her room, don't forget to say, 'Good-morning,' and don't peep into every corner before you do it. (Brothers Grimm, "Little Red-Cap")

The taxi went up the hill, passed the lighted square, then on into the dark, still climbing, then leveled out onto a dark street behind St. Etienne du Mont, went smoothly down the asphalt, passed the trees and standing bus at the Place de la Contrescarpe, then turned onto the cobbles of the Rue Mouffetard. (Ernest Hemingway, *The Sun Also Rises*)

English does not belong to people with virtue, or people with talent, or people who can remember very clearly the difference between a gerund and a gerundive, or people who have succeeded in imitating the affected unregional accents and measured sentences of television announcers. (Jim Quinn, *American Tongue and Cheek*)

It is a place where fast fortunes are made, corporate head-hunting is a profitable sport, and seven-day workweeks send cutting-edge technology tumbling over itself in its competitive rush to the marketplace. (Moiara Johnston, *National Geographic Magazine*)

I admit that I have lost three years of my life to the "twilight zone" of adolescence, where sometimes people get overwhelmed by life in general, where traumas like 'do my shoes go with my belt?'

are terrifying realities that plague young adults daily, and where one surrounds oneself with people who are exceptional partiers, who enjoy good times, and who don't do much of anything else, but finally are your only friends, and are not responsible for your failings. (Lisa Francis, student)

Creatures extrude or vent eggs; larvae fatten, split their shells, and eat them; spores dissolve or explode; root hairs multiply, corn puffs on the stalk, grass yields seed, shoots erupt from the earth turgid and sheathed; wet muskrats, rabbits, and squirrels slide into the sunlight, mewling and blind; and everywhere watery cells divide and swell, swell and divide. (Annie Dillard, *Pilgrim at Tinker Creek*)

I fought migraine then, ignored the warnings it sent, went to school and later to work in spite of it, sat through lectures in Middle English and presentations to advertisers with involuntary tears running down the right side of my face, threw up in washrooms, stumbled home by instinct, emptied ice trays onto my bed and tried to freeze the pain in my right temple, wished only for a neurosurgeon who would do a lobotomy on house call, and cursed my imagination. (Joan Didion, *The White Album*)

Chlor-Timeton is prescribed for hay fever, allergic congestions, conjunctivitis due to allergy, mild forms of hives and swelling due to allergy, prevention of reactions due to transfusions of blood or plasma, hyper-sensitivity of skin due to allergy, follow-up therapy for allergic ractions to drugs. (Edward Stern, *Prescriptive Drugs and Their Side Effects*)

Whether the filmed event is a fruit vendor yelling downstairs for his departed wife, or the fascistic business calls that transpire on the outsized brass bed where a yammering dress designer eats, works, and loves (the only males in sight being the gigantic nudes on the mural behind her bed), the scene most often plays in one take, without development, so that his trademark, *saftig* feistiness, the up-front pugnacity, always hits with more meat than you expect, it claws you with churlish agressions. (Manny Farber and Pat Patterson, "Fassbinder," *Film Comment*)

FULL-BRAIN STYLE 19

My dear Jane, Mr. Collins is a conceited, pompous, narrow-minded, silly man; you know he is, as well as I do; and you must feel, as well as I do, that the woman who marries him, cannot have a proper way of thinking ... You shall not, for the sake of one individual, change the meaning of priniciple and integrity, not endeavor to persuade yourself or me, that selfishness is prudence, and insensibility of danger, security for happiness. (Jane Austen, *Pride and Prejudice*)

So descended the Lem, weird unwieldy flying machine, vehicle on stilts and never before landed, craft with a range of shifting velocities more than comparable to the difference from a racing car down to an amphibious duck, a vehicle with huge variations in speed and handling as it slowed, a vehicle to be flown for the first time in the rapidly changing field of gravity of the moon, going from weightlessness to one-sixth gravity, and one-sixth gravity had never been experienced before in anything but the crudest simulations, and mascons beneath, their location unknown, their effect on moon gravity considerable, angles of vision altering all the time and never near to perfect, the weight of the vehicle reducing drastically as the fuel was consumed, and with it all, the computer guiding them, allowing them to feel all the confidence a one-eyed man can put in a blind man going down a dark alley, and when, at the moment they would take over themselves to fly it manually, a range of choices already tried in simulation but never in realty would be open between full manual and full computer. (Norman Mailer, *Of a Fire on the Moon*)

In the Dining Room, winged chairs upholstered in black denim fauxrose-quartz plastic tiles from the 1950's, and luminous vinyl drapery positioned in a deliberately casual manner, play key roles in establishing an air of fantasy and humor, important elements in the design. (Cameron McKinley, *Architectural Digest*)

But that I am forbid/ To tell the secrets of my prison house,/ I could a tale unfold whose lightest word/ would harrow up thy soul,/ freeze thy young blood,/ Make thy two eyes like stars start from their spheres,/ Thy knotted and combined locks to part,/

And each particular hair to stand on end/ like quills upon the fretful porpentine. (William Shakespeare, *Hamlet*)

TELESCOPING SENTENCES

Telescoping sentences are important because they provide a way to see reality up close. They are enjoyable because they force the writer to look even closer, or consider even more details, than the writer intended when first looking at reality and on first creating the sentence. And as with railroad-ramble, telescoping sentences smooth the flow: they keep details that belong together close together in one sentence.

This is how to make them. The writer spots an object or realizes a general idea: "The rhapis palm sat in a large, white container." This fact must be a complete thought that can work as a finished sentence if left alone. But now, instead of finishing with a period, the writer replaces the period with a comma. The comma must be thought of as a quick turn of a telescopic camera lens that immediately zooms the writer up closer to the material of the original sentence. The writer can zoom up on any part of the "picture" that is already framed by the original sentence. In this example, that means zooming up on either the container or the palm.

For instance, assume the branches of the palm are the detail of interest. Without any word of transition, only a twist of a zoom lens represented by a comma, the sentence can now read: "The rhapis palm sat in a large, white container, the branches stretching into the air..." The writer can place a comma after "air" and zoom up to something framed in this part of the sentence. This time the zoom can only be on the branches or air because the "camera" has focused on them, cutting the overall description of the palm and container out of the picture.

Suppose there is nothing of interest about the air, but the branches have interesting joints or nodes. Zooming in on those, the sentence would now read: "The rhapis palm sat in a large, white container, the branches stretching into the air, fibrous joints knuckling the otherwise smooth surface." The thinking behind building this sentence has worked like this: "The rhapis palm sat in a large, white container, (zoom up closer on the palm) the branches stretching into the air, (zoom up closer on the branches) the fibrous joints knuckling the otherwise smooth surface."

At this point the writer could use a third comma to zoom onto a detail involving the fibrous joints or the smooth surface. Also, by using a comma, one could even "pan" over to another detail on the palm and then start a series of zooms all over again. For instance, the sentence could read: "The rhapis palm sat in a large, white container, the branches stretching into the air, fibrous joints knuckling the otherwise smooth surface, while the palm's green leaves formed zigzag patterns, their surfaces ribbed, capturing the room's left-over dim light."

The major problem with telescoping sentences is that, if the zoomed focuses are described with complete verbs, there is a danger of creating run-ons, a series of complete sentences that should be separated with periods, but that have become spliced together with commas. To avoid this problem, make sure only one part of the sentence has a complete verb. For instance, in the first part of the example sentence "The rhapis palm sat in a large, white container ...," "sat" is the complete verb, but "stretching" in the second part is not because someone cannot go up to someone else and say "the branches stretching into the air." The sentence is therefore not a run-on; it has only one complete verb, "sat." If "were" came before "stretching," the verb of the second part of the sentence would be complete: "The branches were stretching into the air." Then the sentence would be a run-on, killing the validity of the telescoping sentence. Of course, the principles of railroad-ramble may be mixed into telescoping sentences; then as sentence trains are hooked together with connecting words, other complete verbs can legally show up in the sentence.

While trying telescoping sentences, transition words will find their way into the sentences after commas. The resultant sentences are telescoping in spirit even though they are not usually as dramatic as ones using only the comma as zoom lens. For instance, the sentence above could be written thus: "The rhapis palm sat in a large, white container, with its branches stretching into the air, branches that had fibrous joints knuckling the otherwise smooth surface."

WORK OUT

Study the samples below, deciding where telescoping takes place and where railroad-ramble blends in. Then find an interesting area such as a beautiful landscape or an area filled with many different kinds of people, sit down in a comfortable place, and write ten telescoping sentences describing what you see. Number them, since they do not have to be in a unified paragraph or paper. Most of the sentences should be physical descriptions, but try two or three that are telescopic thoughts: a sentence that describes a general idea or opinion the scene brings to mind, then telescopes onto details upon details about this general idea that started the sentence. All ten sentences should have a minimum of two zooms.

SAMPLES

Cathy Smith was waiting at home for her date, reading the new *Seventeen Magazine,* the article about love and romance still simmering in her mind when the doorbell rang. (Michelle Larson, student)

The lane went between back premises — unpainted houses with more of those gay and startling coloured garments on lines, a barn broken-backed, decaying quietly among rank orchard trees, unpruned and weed-choked, pink and white and murmurous with sunlight and with bees. (William Faulkner, *The Sound and the Fury*)

Seeing the radiating minerals is a beautiful visual experience, which is even more fascinating when integrated with your knowledge of nature's submicroscopic happenings, high-energy ultraviolet photons impinging on the surface of the minerals, causing the excitation of atoms in the mineral structure; and

FULL-BRAIN STYLE 23

then the radiation of light frequencies corresponding exactly to the tiny energy-level spacings, and every excited atom emitting its characteristic frequency, with no two different minerals giving off exactly the same color light. (Paul G. Hewitt, *Conceptual Physics*)

The night spot was crowded on Friday night, people stretching across the bar waiting for their drinks, all the people different but alike in their flashiness: the young girls dressed to kill, their clothes in all colors of the rainbow and their pale, cosmetic faces, young and innocent underneath the war-paint; old men tired of their wives, looking for excitement, open shirts revealing gray-haired chests, draped with thick gold plated chains bought at Gemco; middle-aged John Travolta look-alikes, dressed in polyester clothing, spotting the dance floor and bar, looking continuously for admirers, their eyes winking slyly at the women. (Kiki Anderson, student)

When they [the ants] are massed together, all touching, exchanging bits of information held in their jaws like memoranda, they become a single animal. (Lewis Thomas, *The Medusa and the Snail: More Notes of a Biology Watcher*)

Her chauffeur, who had located me for her, he'd popped around the corner to have a drink, which just left this lady and myself, you see, alone, standing underneath this arch, watching all the steamers steaming up, no one about, all quiet on the Western Front, and there she was up against this wall—well, just sliding down the wall, following the blow I'd given her...But...in the end I thought..Aah, why go to all the bother...you know, getting rid of the corpse and all that, getting yourself into a state of tension. (Harold Pinter, *The Homecoming*)

I want everyone in Literature and Language to join our Wednesday morning coffees from 9:30 to noon, Republicans especially, but Democrats too, so long as they are neat and tidy and don't use vulgar language. (Muriel Allingham-Dale, English department coffee hour memo)

But one thing is reassuringly familiar, the girls, twirling prettily in their pleated skirts, dance so much better than their boyfriends, who suffer from a bad case of the clunks. (James Walcott, *New York* magazine)

Anyone appealing to the [ancient Roman] public, informing it upon important affairs, anxious to plead his cause with it or win adherents for his interests, was well advised to use pictures for the purpose. (Arnold Hauser, *The Social History of Art*)

Rain pounded mercilessly upon the shake roof, rushing along the old rain gutters, dripping incessantly from the jagged holes that the rust had eaten in the very thin alloy; and then, as quickly as it had begun, the rain ceased, the sun's rays breaking the dissipated clouds, reaching to reclaim the moisture which had just fallen. (Kevin Bell, student)

He shot the bull four times through the eye. She did not hear the shots but she felt the quake in the huge body as it sank, pulling her forward on its head, so that she seemed, when Mr. Greenleaf reached her, to be bent over whispering some last discovery into the animal's ear. (Flannery O'Connor, "Greenleaf," *Everything that Rises Must Converge*)

If we don't "stop" the child, he develops very little sense of himself, he becomes an automaton, a reflex of the surface of his world playing upon his own surface. (Ernest Becker, *The Denial of Death*)

The handsomest among these Maids of Honour, a pleasant frolicsome girl of sixteen, would sometimes set me astride upon one of her nipples, with many other tricks, wherein the reader will excuse me for not being over particular. (Jonathan Swift, *Gulliver's Travels*)

3
GIVING PAUSE
Ways to slow pace and give punch to quick thoughts

Being able to flow, smoothing together details and thoughts in a natural way, is no more important than being able to stop this flow, give pause, and emphasize special thoughts lost within the flow. Sometimes this pause and emphasis needs to happen after a series of long or middle-length sentences, and other times emphasis or punch is needed in the middle of a sentence itself. The techniques used in chapter 3 are easy to learn, but they are best dramatized and appreciated after the smoothing-the-flow techniques of Chapter 2 become natural to write.

There are many ways to give pause. The following four are important to learn because, to various degrees, they all possess one of the two dimensions essential in all giving-pause techniques: visual attraction and ability to quickly heighten the reader's consciousness. The methods presented here for giving pause are the very short sentence, traditional hieroglyphics, the melted-together-word, and innocent language. Once some of these devices are mastered, you will develop sensitivity to giving pause, and other ways to give pause will evolve over time.

THE VERY SHORT SENTENCE

The three to five word sentence is something we learn to write in the first grade, but ironically it is something that gets flushed from our memories. There are several reasons this happens. Adolescents are mocked for short responses like "yeah," "no," "I don't know," even when those responses are appropriate or accurately depict all the person wants to say. Also, we assume that all thoughts should get more complex as one moves up the educational ladder. By the time a student is in college, his or her mind continuously floods with complex thoughts, thoughts desperately running together masses of details from high-level textbooks and reams of pushed-together class lecture notes. In this overloaded world, a student has to consciously return to the two to five word sentence; it no longer comes to mind naturally. When a student uses it, it seems unexpected. It is surprising. It stops the reader.

Depending on its context, the very short sentence's giving pause has different potentials. When it's content is climactic, it brings the content of descriptive or intellectual flow to a finality. Since a short sentence is unexpected within a smooth flow of writing, it also has the potential to shock and so easily becomes a power tool for content with which to surprise or sting the reader. The very short sentence is also very emphatic, so it is a good container for content that is emphasizing a point about previously written material. Finally, since the very short sentence happens quickly, it helps to give texture and mood to content that is describing something that is fast, terse, or tense.

FULL-BRAIN STYLE 27

WORK OUT
After studying the samples below, return to the smoothing-the-flow sentences you wrote for Chapter 2. Rewrite those sentences and now follow them with a short sentence. Be climactic. Be surprising. Be emphatic. Describe a quick movement or change of thought. But in every case write something that gives pause.

SAMPLES
With proper conditioning, those tiny nerves that lie just under the outer covering of the skin will begin to connect the feeling of moving forward through the water with kicking action. Your baby's skin is a veritable storehouse of information. Help him use it. (Bonnie Prudden, *Your Baby Can Swim*)

For though I am a wholly vicious man / Don't think I can't tell moral tales. I can! (Geoffrey Chaucer, "The Pardoner's Prologue," *The Canterbury Tales*)

Feel the ball, turn it over in your hand; hold it across the seam or the other way, with the seam just to the side of your middle finger. Speculation stirs. You want to get outdoors and throw this spare and sensual object to somebody or, at the very least, watch somebody else throw it. The game has begun. (Roger Angell, *Five Seasons, a Baseball Companion*)

He felt goose pimples clacking all over him as he gazed down despondently at the grim secret Snowden has spilled all over the messy floor. It was easy to read the message in his entrails. Man was matter, that was Snowden's secret. Drop him out a window and he'll fall. Set fire to him and he'll burn. Bury him and he'll rot like other kinds of garbage. The spirit gone, man is garbage. That was Snowden's secret. Ripeness was all. (Joseph Heller, *Catch 22*)

Lawlessness and debauchery accompanied the plague as they had during the great plague of Athens of 430 B.C., when according to Thucydides, men grew bold in the indulgence of pleasure: "for seeing how the rich died in a moment and those who had nothing immediately inherited their property, they reflected that life and riches were alike transitory and they resolved to enjoy themselves while they could." Human behavior is timeless. (Barbara Tuchman, *A Distant Mirror: The Clamitous 14th Century*)

I have neither heard nor read that a Santa Ana [wind] is due, but I know it, and almost everyone I have seen today knows it too. We know it because we feel it. The baby frets. The maid sulks. I rekindle a waning argument with the telephone company, then cut my losses and lie down, given over to whatever it is in the air. (Joan Didion, *Slouching Towards Bethlehem*)

Perhaps they sing to lighten their young hearts, for puce wisps of dusk now coil through the trunks and branches of the thickening forest. Or perhaps they sing to conceal the boy's subterfuge. More likely, they sing for no reason at all, a thoughtless childish habit. To hear themselves. Or to admire their memories. Or to entertain the old man. To fill the silence. Conceal their thoughts. Their expectations. (Robert Coover, "The Gingerbread House," *Pricksongs & Descants*)

This guide will get you started; you'll learn about the brakes and the gas pedal, but you won't be ready for rush hour traffic. That comes with practice. (*The Apple IIc Interactive Owner's Guide*)

Euphorbia Obesa (living-baseball). Spineless globe-shaped succulent with gray and green markings. Very unusual. Widely available. (Ortho's *The World of Cactus & Succulents*)

In the Koran, Allah asks, "The heaven and the earth and all in between, thinkest thou I made them in jest?" It's a good question. (Annie Dillard, *Pilgrim at Tinker Creek*)

She [a female eagle] held still above, buoyed up on the cold current, her crop and hackles gleaming like copper in the sun. The male swerved and sailed. ... He was quicker, tighter in his moves. (Natachee Scott Momaday, *House Made of Dawn*)

FULL-BRAIN STYLE

TRADITIONAL HIEROGLYPHICS

The colon and semicolon are two traditional punctuation marks that have dramatic potential for pauses and they are two eye-catching marks used often by professional writers that are overlooked by students. They are overlooked because their rules of usage are lost in punctuation-pockmarked pages of rhetoric handbooks and also because they are marks that are easy to avoid using. Also, conscientious students who do want to use both marks often confuse them, with good reason since professional writers sometimes use them indiscriminately, or sometimes use them to represent a long-paused comma.

It would be counterproductive in this book to go into all the different rules for the use of each punctuation. There is one good, dramatic usage for each that is worth considering though, an important usage of each that helps to pause the flow.

The colon (:) is used to indicate that either examples or a restatement of the first part of the sentence will now follow in the next part of the sentence. When a writer uses a colon, usually there are no transitional words or verbs to connect the first part of the sentence with the second. Instead there is a blunt pause, giving both halves of the sentence new emphasis. For instance, one can write "Many people chewed the red apple: Bill, my aunt Tina, farmer Olson, and all their cronies." The colon has replaced the transitional phrases like "such as" or "for example." Instead of a smooth flowing of material, the colon creates a dramatic pause that boosts the importance of the people who ate the red apple. The pause gives the start of the list the sharpness of a role call, a sharpness that disappears with the soft blending that the words "such as" would give to the sentence "Many people chewed the red apple, such as, Bill, my aunt Tina, farmer Olson, and all their cronies."

Actually, the most natural, smoothing-the-flow way to write the sentence would be with a railroad-ramble sentence that does not use any transition as follows: "Bill, my aunt Tina, farmer Olson, and all their cronies chewed the red apple." But there is no dramatic pause here. Not only does the list of names not receive special attention as it did in the coloned sentence, but "chewed the red apple" also seems less significant. Before, in the coloned sentence, the fact that "people chewed the red apple" received special focus when the colon cut that fact off with a hard stop, detaching it from the flowing blend of peoples' names.

Two quick side-line notes on the colon: usually the first part of a coloned sentence is a complete sentence, and sometimes writers and printers use a long dash (—) in place of the colon.

The semi-colon (;) should be reserved for an entirely different use than the colon. Among its many uses, the most dramatic is to replace a conjunction or "hooking" word such as "and," "but," "nor," "or," "yet," "so," and "for." In the sentence, "They did not just eat the red apple; they pulverized it," "they pulverized it" takes on an intensity and emphasis that would be missed in a smoother flowing sentence: "They did not just eat the apple, but they pulverized it."

Sometimes it is a must to use the semi-colon as a substitute for "ands" or commas that separate a series of items because commas are already being used to telescope on each one of the items in the series as discussed in chapter 2. The sentence would become too confusing to read if commas were to be used to both separate the items in the series as well as to telescope on each one. For instance, in the following sentence, each of the different ways the cronies worked on their apples is telescoped on with commas, so each of the different ways is separated from each other with semicolons. "All the cronies worked on their apples: they polished them, first spitting on them, rubbing the skins as hard as they could; chopped them, using sharp, machete-like blades, rusted after years of neglect; chewed them, the cronies' teeth buckling on contact with the apples' hardness, apple skin slivering into their gums; and pulverized them, using all the energy left in their jaw muscles." If this sentence had used commas where there are semicolons, each action would have been confused with any previous telescoping.

FULL-BRAIN STYLE

WORK OUT

Write an essay about something you are ether very annoyed with or very happy about. To hold onto your flowing anger or ecstasy, use long, smoothing-the-flow sentences, including telescoping sentences that use semi-colons like the last example. Then climax thoughts with very short sentences. Use colons and semi-colons throughout to create emotional intensity. Before starting, study the following samples. Remember, sometimes a long dash (—) is used in place of a colon.

SAMPLES

Everyone also remembers a few of the observances of childhood — wishing on the first star; looking at the new moon over the right shoulder; avoiding the cracks in the sidewalk on the way to school while chanting, "Step on a crack, break your mother's back"; wishing on white horses, on loads of hay, on covered bridges, on red cars; saying quickly, "Bread-andbutter" when a post or a tree separated you from the friend you were walking with. (Margaret Mead, *A Way of Seeing*)

The demand for circuses, and when the milder spectacles are still insufficiently life-arousing, the demand for sadistic exploits and for blood is characteristic of civilizations that are losing their grip: Rome under the Caesars, Mexico at the time of Montezuma, Germany under the Nazis. (Lewis Mumford, *Technics and Civilization*)

Representation is a game, which proceeds even if we forget that in this game all our dealings with the world are at stake. Here is an image. It is as simple as it can be. It consists of three elements: a uniformly salmon colored background and in it two objects: a glass of water and an umbrella. (Bernard Noel, *Magritte*)

Lanegrin's equation for motion therefore has its roots in two worlds: the macroscopic world represented by the diagonal force and the microscopic world represented by the fluctuating, or Brownian force. (Bernard Lavends, *Scientific America*)

It is not the games children play in the evening that I want to speak of now, it is of a contemporaneous atmosphere that has little to do with them; that of the fathers of families, each in his space of lawn, his shirt fishlike pale in the unnatural light and his face nearly anonymous, hosing their lawns. (James Agee, *A Death in the Family*)

Darwin, however, noted that whole classes of continental life were absent from the island; that certain plants which were herbvaceous (non-woody) on the mainland had developed into trees on the islands; that island animals often differed from their counterparts on the mainland. (Loren Eiseley, *Scientific America*)

Life's but a walking shadow, a poor player/ That struts and frets his hour upon the stage/ And then is heard no more: it is a tale/ Told by an idiot, full of sound and fury,/ Signifying nothing. (William Shakespeare, *Macbeth*)

You have, I think, a gift for bringing up children: you could, I am sure, have been of use to a human being of your own kind with your methods; such a person would have seen the reasonableness of what you told him ... (Franz Kafka, *Letter to His Father*)

THE MELTED-TOGETHER WORD

There are many words in English that are made by melting together other words with hyphens. For instance, the words "blue" and "green" mean two different colors but when they are melted with a hyphen into a third word, "blue-green," we have a whole new concept, a whole new color. Most student writers do not realize they can melt together as many words as they would like as long as this new made-up word functions as one word in the structure of a sentence. These made up words, by their uniqueness and heavy load of content, and often by their cleverness, slow the sentence flow down and focus attention on their content. Fresh, original, hyphen-created words are fun and offer opportunities for wit. Since hyphen-created words often contain enough material for a complete sentence, they become show-stoppers and bring the reader's attention to their content, content that might be blended away if the material in the hyphenated word were relegated to its own, separate sentence.

The following sentence makes nice use of the melted-together word: "Farmer Olson had a here-I-come, I-love-life attitude which gave everyone a pat-on-the-back feeling." Note that "here-I-come" and "I-love-life" cannot be connected by a hyphen since they work independently from one another. Any melted together chunk of words that functions as one word in the sentence, in this case as an adjective, must be broken off as a separate word. Do not write "here-I-come-I-love-life."

On the other hand, to test whether or not a phrase can be hyphenated in the first place, the writer simply removes the hyphenated word and replaces it with a single word. For instance, "here-I-come" could be replaced with any number of single word adjectives such as "exuberant" or "bubbly," and "I-love-life" could be replaced by "positive" or "optimistic." If the writer cannot replace the hyphenated word with a single word, then the hyphenated word is not functioning as a single word in the sentence structure and the words must remain as single, unmelted words. Melted-together words are almost always adjectives, sometimes nouns.

Melted-together words are not just more fun to use than thesaurus-dug-out words; they are usually more exacting. For instance, in terms of meaning, in the sentence above, "I-love-life" might easily be replaced by the word "positive," but "here-I-come" includes much more about the person's mental attitude and outward mannerisms than most single word choices could suggest.

A student who has trouble arriving at original hyphenated words should simply write a sentence followed by one or more sentences on the first sentence's subject. For instance, a student might write "Today farmer Olson put up some kitchen shelves. They looked easy to put up but they turned out to be troublesome." Next the writer can try taking complete or incomplete phrases from the second sentence, melt them together, and use them as a single word adjective in the first sentence. The result might be the following: "Today farmer Olson put up some they-looked-real-easy, turned-out-to-be-troublesome kitchen shelves." Note there is no comma between "troublesome" and "kitchen" just as there would be no comma between any other adjectives or nouns.

WORK OUT

Creative hyphenated words are powerful and unusual; most professionals use them sparingly. But learning to use them is fun and they provide a unique way to give form to what might otherwise seem unexplainable. Study the following examples and then try writing ten sentences that have at least one original, melted-together word. Remember, if you have problems thinking of material for a melted-together word, write a second sentence about the first sentence you create, then try turning the second sentence into a melted-together word by placing it in the first sentence.

SAMPLES

Are you aware of a fact-that-should-be-startling about the High Days of my youth? All were Europe-rooted or American-rooted. Not one celebration in my black household or in any black household that I knew featured any black glory or greatness or grandeur. (Gwendolyn Brooks, *A Report from Part One*)

...[Elizabeth] Drew is a member of the there-are-no-easy answers school of discourse, though she tends to favor the royal "we." (James Walcott, *Vanity Fair*)

One young woman described the problem to her encounter group thus: "I feel like I'm contradictory ... and people keep hitting me with the you're-not-what-you-seem issue, and it's really wearing me down..." (Kenneth Gergen, *Psychology Today*)

Skyway Systems is in high gear with just-in-time trucking. (Roger Neal, *Forbes Magazine*)

FULL-BRAIN STYLE 35

Essentially, this is a movie about Jesssica Lange's spirit-of-the-prairie face. (Pauline Kael, *The New Yorker*)

As one delves deeper and deeper into ETIQUETTE, disquieting thoughts come. That old Is-It-Worth-It Blues starts up again, softly, perhaps, but plainly. Those who have mastered etiquette, who are entirely, impeccably right, would seem to arrive at a point of exquisite dullness. (Dorothy Parker, "Mrs. Post Enlarges on Etiquette")

Gazing down at the street, he became confused as to the problem beneath the question: was it, is-it-me-who-called-[Rabbi]-Binder-a-bastard? or, is-it-me-prancing-around-on-the-roof? ... Yakov Blotnik's old mind hobbled slowly, as if on crutches, and though he couldn't decide precisely what the boy was doing on the roof, he knew it wasn't good — that is, it wasn't-good-for-the-Jews. For Yakov Blotnik life had fractionated itself simply: things were either good-for-the-Jews or no-good-for-the-Jews. (Philip Roth, "The Conversion of the Jews")

She couldn't recall the precise moment she began to feel resentful of the hand-shake-only goodnights, of the moist, cold, kiss-on-the-forehead routine, but she suddenly found herself unable to think of anything but how she could seduce him. (Olga Blohm, student)

Hate needs no instruction, but waits only to be provoked ... hate, ... that invisible tongue-tripper, that unkempt finger in every pie, that sudden oh-so-curiously chilling look — could it be boredom? — on your dear one's features, making them quite ugly. (Katherine Anne Porter, "The Necessary Enemy")

Like most daytime dramas, CBS's "Love of Life" simply sketches in a Dirty Secret, leaving the details up to our overheated steam-on-the-windshield imaginations. (James Wolcott, *The Village Voice*)

INNOCENT LANGUAGE

Another way to bring attention to detail within a smooth flow of writing is to change words or phrases into more graphic, elemental, and truthful terms than the reader expects to find. To do this the writer assumes an innocent, almost child-like, state of mind that questions the validity of all words, and the concepts they represent, no matter how simple those words seem to be. This questioning can only take place when a writer intimately understands or mentally visualizes the reality that a concept and its word stand in for. Innocent language is consciousness-raising the same way children are when they dismiss the sophistications and complexities of the adult world, speak directly, and flush out truths that adults have camouflaged in their own subconscious.

For example, the words "cow," "door," and "apple" are not too simple for innocent language treatment. The word "apple" seems abstract compared to the more physical, elemental, and truthful phrase "shiny, red seed pod." Innocent language sounds playful, but it is not child's play: the writer in this case needs to know what an apple truthfully is, what it really is in the botanical world. The effect of innocent language on the reader can be stunning. For instance, if the sentence, "Bill, my aunt Tina, farmer Olson, and all their cronies, chewed the red apple," is changed to "Bill, my aunt Tina, farmer Olson, and all their cronies, chewed the shiny, red seed pod," the reader needs to give more than just pause. In this case, the reader is startled, realizing the people in the sentence are not just country friends who share food; they are full-fledged herbivores, animals sharing the plant world with other animals. Our superiority over animals is momentarily knocked out from under us. This stunning truth gives pause, not to mention the pause created by the unusual terminology for apple.

Similarly, a "wood slab with hinges" makes a door seem less permanent and a "large animal with a pink bag on its stomach" makes a cow a bulkier and more grotesque version of a grazing animal than we would normally visualize. Innocent language never leaves room for the reader to escape the physicality of a situation, thing, or concept; it always calls attention to itself by surprising, if not shocking the reader. The more abstract, intellectual, or sophisticated the tone of the ongoing flow in a piece

FULL-BRAIN STYLE

of writing, the more abruptly the injection of innocent language gives pause, and focuses attention on its content. Innocent language does not compare unlike things; that is a metaphor. It does not make reality more intellectual or sophisticated; that is euphemism. Innocent language works by speaking too clearly. Innocent language has to do with taking the literal to an extreme, sometimes a humorous extreme.

Not many writers make use of this subtle technique for giving pause, but it constitutes a grammatical principle that expands a writer's consciousness into another dimension of perceiving and using language that is lost on dictionary-digging writers. This is true even if in reality a writer finally rejects innocent language choices in his final draft. When a writer is aware of the possibilities of innocent language, all language comes under playful scrutiny and so expression indirectly becomes clearer. In a sense, no regularly used traditional grammatical principle can equal the importance of innocent language, let alone be able to bring the freshness to writing that innocent language can bring when it is used.

WORK OUT

The best way to test the use of innocent language is to examine a page of nonfictional writing that takes itself seriously, such as an etiquette book, a cookbook, or a college textbook, and rewrite it, changing a word or concept in every other line into innocent language. Remember, innocent language is not an informal way of talking about something; it involves thinking about both the most sophisticated and the most simplistic words in terms of their lowest common denominator of truth. This truth is usually more graphic and more shocking than the vocabulary word that has evolved to replace the truth. Innocent language carries the reader back to a reality that becomes lost with maturity. First study the following sentences. The innocent language words or phrases are in italics.

SAMPLES

The following examples of innocent language by Mitford and Ellison might be considered to be metaphors (see chapter 4), but in the context of the rest of the sentence, and in context of the works they are taken from, the words can be read as literal truths.

Jones is next wheeled into the appointed slumber room where a few touches may be added — his favorite pipe placed in his hand or, if he was a great reader, a book propped into position. . . . Here he will *hold open house* for a few days, visiting hours 10 A.M. to 9 P.M. (Jessica Mitford, *The American Way of Death*)

"Nonlectures" One: I & My Parents" (E.E. Cummings, *i:Six Nonlectures IX*)
swims-carrying-stick: beaver
long-claws: grizzly bear
bird-who-carries-mud-in-mouth: swallow
lump-raiser: mosquito
(Ruth Beebe Hill, "Idiomatic Phrases" in *Hanta Yo*)

I am an *invisible man*. No, I am not a spook like those who haunted Edgar Alan Poe . . . I am invisible, understand, simply because people refuse to see me. (Ralph Ellison, *Invisible Man*)

I'm sick of peering at the world through false eyelashes, so everything I see is mixed with a shadow of *bought hairs;* I'm sick of weighting my head with a *dead mane,* unable to move my neck freely, terrified of rain, or wind, of dancing too vigorously in case I sweat into my *lacquered* curls. (Germaine Greer, *The Female Eunuch*)

There is no question that there is an unseen world. The problem is, *how far is it from midtown and how late is it open?* (Woody Allen, *The New Yorker Magazine*)

As Aristotle put it, the beginning of philosophy is wonder. I am simply amazed to find myself living on a *ball of rock* that swings around an immense *spherical fire* . . . But what really gets me is that almost all the substance of this maze [of life], aside from water, was once other living bodies — the bodies of animals and

FULL-BRAIN STYLE

plants — and that I had to obtain it by *murder* . . . I exist solely through membership in this perfectly weird arrangement of beings that flourish by *chewing each other up*. (Alan Watt, *Does It Matter?*)

Although the two [eternities of darkness before and after life] ae identical twins, man, as a rule, views the prenatal abyss with more calm than the one he is heading for *(at some forty-five hundred heartbeats an hour)*. (Vladimir Nabokov, *Speak, Memory*)

Gerber dismisses the Stages line as a copy of its own color-coded system, which differentiates the *mush* from the *chunks* but does not organize the food according to the baby's age. (Jaclyn Fierman, *Fortune Magazine*)

In World War I they [engineers] made *a machine that would throw five hundred pounds of steel fifty miles.* (Andy Rooney, *An Essay on War*)

4

FINE TUNING REALITY
Ways to spark interest in truth with metaphor

Essentially there are two kinds of languages that we all use: literal and metaphoric. Literal language is straight-forward, dictionary-defined language that is essential to living and survival. When we approach a stop sign, we want a direct, clear, quickly understood message to stop. We would think twice about driving streets where we knew drivers would encounter varied, ambiguous, interesting messages at each stop sign they came to: "Cool your fire" one time, "plug the four-corner gap" another time, and "give sacrifice to the god of pause" the next time. If someone yelled "fire" in a theatre, we would curse language if, on being calm enough to actually look for an exit sign, we

FULL-BRAIN STYLE

spotted messages like "yawning wall" or "body window," but even the panic of finding these messages would be a luxury if instead of "fire," we initially heard "the evil gods finally fart on me," or "heat tumbles over the building like a liquid sun."

These ambiguous, varied messages are from the metaphoric world. Although undesirable in the above situations, in other situations metaphor has the ability to do something that literal, dictionary-defined language cannot do. In one flash, metaphor is capable of simultaneously informing in three different ways: it loads many meanings or associations into a reader's mind, makes the complicated or unexplainable clearer, and excites the reader's interest in what is being written about. In short, metaphor fine-tunes writing and fuels it. Because it does, it is essential to all kinds of writing, most noticeably to literature, song, and journalism, but also to correspondence and analytic writing in business, social science, the arts, theology, politics, and even biological and physical sciences.

For instance, while reading *Science Digest*'s thorough survey of a few years ago that located and described the work of America's top 100 scientists under the age of forty, one finds that these top molecular biologists, biochemists, astrophysicists, computer scientists, and theoretical physicists riddled the descriptions of their work with metaphor: objects with strong gravitational pulls are "white dwarfs" and "black holes," axes of galaxies behave "like those of a football slightly squashed," the developing brain is "like a printed circuit being wired," isotopes "tailor plutonium," computers should do what a person means and not what they are told, "like apprentice carpenters and not like hammers," electrons bunch up "like the compressed areas of a slinky," and biologists try to control "food webs" while high energy physicists grapple with "ink-jet."

So metaphor fine-tunes all writing, and in order to become a good writer, to enjoy writing and feel in control of language, aside from smoothing-the-flow and giving-pause, the most important stylistic principle to learn is fine-tuning with metaphor. Most would-be writers resist this fact because they lack confidence in their ability to create anything other than dead, cliche metaphors or they do not believe that metaphor is essential to good writing. Often, just a definition of metaphor alarms student writers. For one thing, an explanation of how metaphor works always sounds like an absurd riddle or mathematical corollary.

For instance, it is natural to plead mental anguish when told that metaphor informs by comparing something to be understood or to be revitalized to a second thing that in some crucial ways is like the first thing to be understood or revitalized, but in other crucial ways is very different from that thing. Nevertheless, it is exactly this unusual informing through both similarities and dissimilarities, taking place all in the same breath, that makes metaphor a powerful communications tool.

The best way to recognize how much we actually live and often thrive in a metaphorical language-world is through an examination of slang. Slang is a creative, vital area of language acquired naturally, without academic scaffolds and braces, by young children, high school and college students, and other groups, so it offers an ideal starting point for an appreciation of metaphor. The first unit here, "Slang Hang," bold-prints some of this everyday metaphor and also suggests a way that a slang frame of mind can help a writer be original with metaphor.

Even slang can become cliche, and when metaphors die from over-use, we tend to skip over them mentally. For instance, at one time "broken-hearted" might have been an effective metaphor. Maybe with certain inflections in the voice, lovers or songs using this metaphor could still make it effective. But in a written piece this metaphor is usually too easy for the reader to tune out and it is necessary for the writer to be more inventive. The two units, "Body Parts" and "Line Ups," provide ways to be original with metaphors despite one's lack of creativity. The unit entitled "Mixed Masters" does this too, but also demonstrates, through a follow-up work out, how metaphors are economical and informative.

FULL-BRAIN STYLE

SLANG HANG

Youth's language creativity grows on slang that is metaphoric. For over thirty years rock music has had periods of time when there were several rock stars that filled their lyrics with complicated expressions of love and related matters communicated through rich use of metaphor, much of it slang. Metaphorical lyrics come and go in such a fury in the rock world that for most students under twenty this year's favorite lyrics will be ancient history in six months. Shock-valued slang stays around longer and fuels the language of youth from the later elementary years into the early years of college. A recent inquiry of college freshman brought forth the following metaphoric slang: fur-burger, break wind, wrinkled-neck pigeon, main vein, lung cookies (phlegm), parallel parking, smells like something crawled up your ass and died, and choke my chicken. Obviously these do not measure up to everyone's literary or moral sense of decorum, but neither do some of those from Chaucer's characters, like his Bible-clerks who take pride in telling of an opportunity to "grind their corn." The point is, this obscene slang informs through similarities and dissimilarities. Some might question whether they load several associations into the reader's mind and renew interest in what is being talked about. For a youthful audience not haunted by adults, they do.

Business people are just as surprised to find that metaphoric slang is the language world they love to play in too. The cartoonist Gary Trudeau dramatized this love of kitsch metaphor several years ago when for a few weeks "Doonesbury" frames were peppered with the slang of a motion picture business deal: "we're looking at a package that's going to make this town weep," "when word hits the street the majors will break down our doors," "he'd play the damn car if he had to," "if you cross him he'll crush you and send you back to Kansas," "your boy is putting me away," "Would that be a coup? Is this man a complete maniac?," "I hate to put the arm on you babe," "Then we're talking green light?," "You ran it up the flagpole and the money saluted?," "The money loved it," "Bottom line time," "Sweet?," "Don't play hardball with me, you old hack!," "Come to Pappa you little maniac!"

These expressions, like most slang words and phrases, are metaphoric. The main difference between metaphoric slang and other metaphors is that slang is usually intended to be understood by a smaller, inside group; therefore the comparision the metaphor is making is deliberately more obscure, or at least it seems to be, in an attempt to discourage outsiders from listening in. But once someone is given the code, told what the slang word means, it quickly makes metaphoric sense. For instance, a number of years ago the New York police department used the slang word "a hook." It is almost impossible to figure out this metaphor, but as soon as one knows that a hook is someone of higher office that can do favors for others beneath him, especially in terms of pulling one up through promotions, "a hook" becomes a fitting metaphor. Likewise, not many can figure out what is meant when a waitress says "Stretch a crowd of suds and let them walk," but when explained that "stretch" refers to pulling the suction levers for carbonated drinks, "a crowd" refers to three of an item (two's company), "suds" refers to beer or rootbeer, and "let them walk" refers to packaging so that the food can be taken from the restaurant, the metaphors sparkle.

Since slang is always to some extent secretive, it is fun to use and almost always makes written and oral discourse more playful. In fact, slang is so powerful, at times it makes many mundane, uneventful endeavors and conversations tolerable, making language interesting when the subject at hand is routine at best. But other times slang actually can fill a language void, giving a name to a new situation or item that never received its own label. For instance, many of the words in Rich Hall and Friends' book entitled *Sniglets,* a listing of words that do not appear in the dictionary, could be considered a version of slang. Examples include "bumperglints," the small reflective obstacles in the middle of highways that warn drivers of a dividing line, "expressholes," people who violate the rules of a eight-items-or-less line, "cinemuck," the sticky combination of sweets and trash that cover movie theatre floors, and "hozone," the place where one sock in every laundry load disappears.

FULL-BRAIN STYLE 45

WORK OUT

Getting into a slang-creating frame of mind is one of the best ways to originate interesting metaphor for a piece of writing. A successful way to dramatize that anyone is capable of getting into that frame of mind is through the following amusing exercise. First list ten items, events, or kinds of people associated with a given profession or endeavor. Being a student could be considered a profession and it might be fun to think of being a son, daughter, mother, or father as a specific endeavor.

Now opposite each item in the list hang a slang word or phrase that is totally original. The only criteria is that these slang words are metaphoric, fun to use, and maybe slightly obscure in meaning without previously knowing their definitions, but are very clear once those definitions are known. Also, the slang should not sound like anything currently in operation. After each slang word and definition, try writing a sentence using the slang word. Following is an example of lists from three student writers:

Automobile Mechanic

tune-up a thunderbird:	ressurect the chicken radiator
work on a pick-up truck:	cold shower the cowboy
tune-up the transmission:	unhitch the get-along
new brakes for a large car:	plug the boat

Football

a religious quarterback:	a Bible chucker
an intellectual coach:	a wire head
pulling guards:	hoof skippers
a pass thrown too hard to handle:	a sternum sticker

Student

tough professor:	a bubble burster
an instructor that requires much reading:	a page warrior
boring professors:	yawners
expensive books:	check bouncers

BODY PARTS

One way to create original metaphors is to take any object whatsoever, break it into its separate parts, and then connect those different parts to the one literal word in a sentence that needs to be clarified or energized. The connection between the parts and the one literal word can be done with the word "of" or through the use of the possessive ('s). At least one of these connections usually proves to be a useful metaphor.

In the following example, a student took different items from a sporting goods store and connected each one with "her friends'" in the sentence "Sue is her friends' _____ at work." The student thought about the implications of each sport's item and then, after each sentence defined the metaphor.

Sue is her friends' *soccer ball* at work. (Whenever anything goes wrong at work, Sue is the first to be blamed and to take abuse. She is constantly being transferred to different departments or assignments.)

Sue is her friends' *tennis racket* at work. (Sue controls her friends, convincing them to do what she wants, and positioning them in different parts of the company.)

Sue is her friends' *scuba tank* at work. (Sue teaches the new employees everything so that they are 100% dependent on her, and without her they would not be able to function in their new working environment.)

Sue is her friends' *main sail* at work. (Sue is the only one that can take a great amount of stress and keep going, thinking out solutions slowly and calmly and with tremendous confidence.)

There is another way to use body parts. Again, break any object down into parts and this time use those noun parts as verbs in a sentence. The following student listed as many parts of a car as he could think of and then wrote the following sentences and definitions.

FULL-BRAIN STYLE

He *filtered* his way to the top. (He was able to promote himself, standing out above the others, by publicizing his achievments and working hard, finally being recognized and advanced to the top.)

He *geared* his way to the top. (Through careful timing and cautious, almost imperceptible political advances, he gradually made his way to the top.)

He *spark-plugged* his way to the top. (He made it to the top because of his energy and ability to excite and motivate his peers.)

He *mufflered* his way to the top. (He made his way to the top by hiding his deceitful past and not calling attention to his faults.)

In a paper, about "Sue" or "he" from the above examples, the writer might only use one of the metaphors discovered through body parts. But possibly the other metaphors could work well with other people discussed in the paper, or give the writer new subtopics or directions for the paper. All the metaphors in each set above will also work well together to unify the paper since they are extensions of one another, all coming from the same object or place.

WORK OUT

The best way to practice body parts, is to think of one subject to be written about literally, and another object that will be broken into parts to be used as a metaphor the way sporting goods and car were used above. Other possibilities could include parts of a computer, parts of an insect, parts of religious rituals, ingredients of a cooking recipe, or parts of the novel. Connect five of these parts using "of" or the possessive to the literal subject in the manner the first student did above. Next turn five of the parts into verbs as the second student did. Then either define each of the metaphors or use five of them in a very short paper. The results are fun and always surprising.

LINE UPS

Another way to originate metaphors, is to take a noun and line up different adjectives in front of it that normally would not be used because they do not make literal sense with that particular noun. For instance, there is nothing metaphoric about a red apple or a hard apple. But what about a loquacious apple, or a lawless apple, or an intense apple, or an insane apple, an ingratiating apple, a dressy apple, a cosmic apple, a business-like apple, an amatory apple? These are all metaphors. Following are student examples of line ups:

demented rain	purple attitude	pungent novel
bashful rain	melted attitude	impotent novel
ecstatic rain	knarled attitude	elastic novel
licentious rain	terminal attitude	sculptured novel

Once these writers created these metaphors, they tried to define them. For instance, "demented rain" is a rain with no rhythm, sporadically pouring forcefully, then sprinkling lightly, at times crashing down loudly; "bashful rain" comes from an ominously dark sky that promises gushes of rain, but the rain itself is less than a light sprinkle; a "terminal attitude" is a dangerous attitude that inevitably will lead its bearer into a situation that will disrupt his or her whole life.

WORK OUT

As with body parts, the best exercise is simply to make lists involving a repeated concept or word that is to be taken as literal, proceed it each time with different "impossible" adjectives, and then try to define the resulting metaphors. Preceding inanimate, physical items with adjectives reserved for living things, always yields instant metaphor. After defining each metaphor, the student writer should try using the metaphor in a written sentence.

MIX MASTERS

One game-like way to create inventive metaphors, almost in spite of one's lack of creativity, involves mixing words into sentences

FULL-BRAIN STYLE

through rules that force one of the words to become a metaphor. There are several things to learn from playing the game, including the potential of all words to become useful metaphors and the power inherent in turning some nouns into verbs to create metaphors. A follow-up work out in this unit provides a convincing process to carefully discover all the implications of any metaphor and realize how efficient metaphors are. But first the fun part.

WORK OUT

Mix-mastered sentences are created under rigid mixing rules. The writer creates the sentence by combining three entries at random from a list that is already a mixture of basically noun items, so first a list of interesting nouns needs to be assembled.

The most meaningful way to do this is to list at least twenty-five names, titles, or items that are or have been important to the writer's life. In order to stimulate the imagination, it might be helpful to think of five nouns the writer associates with smell, five with vision, five with sound, five with times or places, five with movements, or five with taste or touch. The entries may actually be more than one word if they are titles of songs, books, restaurants, or films.

Once the list is made the entries should be written on separate pieces of scrap paper or note cards, then mixed up. A typical list might include entries such as the following: honeysuckle, candle flame, rain, weightlifting, gasoline, Ted's Hideway, gossip, heater, black Japanese pine, MACBETH. Next the cards are shuffled, three are drawn at random, and the writer has thirty seconds to write a sentence using all three, but under these rigid rules: (l) the writer may change the form of the three random words, (2) the writer may use any number of articles ("a" and "the") but only one preposition, and (3) the writer may add any other word whatsoever, but only one such word. (4) Finally, when finished, the sentence must have at least one metaphor and even the whole sentence can be metaphorical with only limited literal force.

These sentences must be created quickly, within about thirty seconds per sentence, because this limits the rational, left brain's chance to interfere in the playful mixing. One of the most important things to do in creating these sentences is to try and use one of the nouns as a verb. This not only cuts time but also, if this noun is one that never has a verb form, the writer will automatically create the required metaphor.

This is an amusing game to play in groups of three or four with everyone sharing the same three words from one of the writers each time, then reading the sentences aloud to one another, comparing the different results each writer has created with the same words. Most of the sentences will be accidentally amusing or exotic. Sentences that are incomplete, or are literal without metaphoric sense, or that break the rules, should be struck out. Words from the random word list should be underlined.

Following are some typical mixes created in less than thirty seconds each: "The boy *freewayed* through *high school dances*." "The *cigarettes flowered* the *loud music*." "A *hummingbird candle-flamed* the autumn *breeze*." "*Lemon verbena gossiped* with *mowed grass*."

FOLLOW-UP WORK OUT

It is fairly easy to mix-master these metaphors, although some sentences usually will work out better than others. However, it is another matter to understand the true worth of what has been created by these mixing "accidents." Trying to understand what has happened in creating these metaphoric sentences is one of the best ways to appreciate metaphoric efficiency. To understand involves a three step process. (1) The first step is to write down the mix-mastered sentence.

(2) The second step is to identify all the metaphors in the sentence and, after each one, list all the universal, basic associations that word has when it is used as a literal word, before given metaphorical life. This must be done by isolating that word and considering its literal meanings and universal characteristics

FULL-BRAIN STYLE 51

without looking at the mix-mastered, metaphoric sentence in which the word now exists. Also, if the writer anticipates how the word will translate in step 3 at this point, too many implictions of the metaphor will be unrealized.

(3) In the third step, the writer looks at both step one and two in order to write a literal sentence that replaces all metaphors from step one with as many words or spin-offs of words from step two as possible. Sometimes words from step two can replace the metaphor by simply inserting them into the step-one sentence in place of the metaphor. Usually though, a certain amount of creative spin-off from the associations of step two is a necessity. Since the metaphor is loaded with meanings or implications, translating it will result in a more involved sentence than the original sentence of step 1 where the metaphor had compressed all those meanings.

Below are two student writer examples, followed by an explanation of how one of them moved from step two to three, the most difficult, but telling transition.

step one: Lemon verbena gossiped with mowed grass.
step two: gossip — verbal, secretive, usually about something personal that is untruthful or unkind, the information changes drastically as it is passed along.
step three: Lemon verbena barely touched the mowed grass, sometimes obscuring it from view or actually damaging it, other times sticking to another plant, changing its appearance.

step one: A humming bird candle-flamed the autumn breeze.
step two: candle-flame — bright, red, blue, flickering; burns on a wick enclosed in wax; small
step three: A small humming bird, surrounded by darkness, flew through the autumn breeze, the breeze ruffling the bird's feathers as it flew, causing the feathers to sparkle many shades of crimson and blue as they were struck at different angles by the fading light.

In regard to the first student sentence, the student realized that her sentence of step three had to be about "lemon verbena" doing something with "mowed grass." That is what the original literal part of her mixmastered sentence was about. The "doing something" part of the sentence is the part the metaphor "gossiped" covered before, but now must be replaced with something literal. That something will necessarily be complicated because there are several associations loaded into the word "gossiped" discovered and listed above in step two, and they are elaborate. To write a literal sentence, the student can do whatever is necessary to replace the metaphor with these associations, including changing the sentence's syntax and doing creative spin-offs. Moving from step two to step three takes imagination and inventiveness.

In step three, the student has spun "barely touched" off of "whisper" listed in step two, has paralleled "obscuring it from view or actually damaging it" with "untruthful and unkind" listed in step two, and equivocated "changing its appearance" with "information can change drastically as it is passed along" listed above in step two. The literal force of the original sentence, lemon verbena doing something to the mowed grass, has not been altered.

The true test as to whether the student has discovered a good translation, is to read the translated sentence next to the mixmastered sentence and ask whether they sound like they mean the same thing. "Lemon verbena barely touched the mowed grass, sometimes obscuring it from view or actually damaging it, other times sticking to another plant, changing its appearance." "Lemon verbena gossiped with mowed grass." The two sentences seem to be close translations of one another. The student had no idea what the metaphor "gossiped" implied when creating the original sentence, or even in doing step two. Not only are those implications clearer after step three, but the economy and complexity inherent in the metaphor "gossip" are dramatically realized.

FULL-BRAIN STYLE 53

SAMPLES

Since metaphors are often combinations of body parts, line ups, and mix masters, professional examples of all three have been combined and listed here. Many times good metaphors blend into a piece of writing, registering their load of meanings, associations, clarifications, and vitality on the subconscious part of a reader's mind. They are italicized here for ease of identification in studying them.

You ain't nothing but a *hound dog,* . . . You never *caught a rabbit* and you ain't no friend of mine. (Elvis Presley, "Hound Dog")

He [Thomas Rowland] *punctures* pretensions by lengthening a nose or exaggerating a paunch and sets up an *undertow of commentary* in vignettes acted out by *domestic animals.* Cognoscenti and connoisseurs get the *back of his hand,* while gluttons seem destined to *drown* in their orgies. (Suzanne Muchnic, The Los Angeles Times)

She is an *answer* rather than a *question,* a *vibrant and easily worked material* that is *shaped by* the imagination and sensuality of the male. (Octavio Paz, The Labyrinth of Solitude)

The high *grey-flannel* fog of winter closed off the Salinas Valley from the sky and from all the rest of the world. (John Steinbeck, "The Chrysanthemums")

He's (John McLaughlin) the show's *tower of power,* its *smokestack of indignation,* its *mad mullah.* He uses his *hanging-judge voice as a gavel, rapping the show to disorder* and demanding a *strict verdict* ... (James Walcott, Vanity Fair)

The *tigers of wrath* are wiser than the *horses of instruction.* (William Blake, The Marriage Between Heaven and Hell)

Football is a game consisting of blocking and tackling and not much else. But it is the duty of those who promote it and have a stake in it to invest it with the trappings and *liturgical cant of an occult Eastern religion.* (Jim Murray, The Los Angeles Times)

The gates of academe open each spring, and thousands of newly anointed artists and art historians tramp into the city, *pushing their paper degrees before them in wheelbarrows, like Weimer Germans out to buy a loaf of bread.* (Kay Larson, New York Magazine)

And he [Samson] said to them [the Philistines], "If you had not *plowed with my heifer,* you would not have found out my riddle." (*The Old Testament*)

Nothing about him indicated intelligence except two cold clinical *nickel-colored* eyes that *hung* with a *motionless curiosity* over whatever he looked at. (Flannery O'Connors, "The Enduring Chill")

There were *freckled* places on the ground where the light sifted down through the leaves, and the *freckled* places *swapped* about a little, showing there was a little breeze up there. (Mark Twain, *The Adventures of Huckleberry Finn*)

Evolution is still an infinitely long and tedious biologic *game,* with only the winners *staying at the table,* but the rules are beginning to look more flexible. We live in a *dancing* matrix of viruses; they dart, rather *like bees,* from organism to organism ... transplanting grafts of DNA, passing around heredity *as though at a great party.* (Lewis Thomas, *The Lives of a Cell: Notes of a Biology Watcher*)

Public opinion is a *weak tyrant* compared with our own private opinion. (Henry David Thoreau, *Walden*)

So an acquisition involving the blemished Harvester...could solve Ketelsen's case dilemma while providing just the *shark repellent* he needs to maintain the conglomerate's independence. (J. Ellis and J. Norman, *Businessweek*)

Live on *broken phrases* and *syllable gristle,* telegraphese and film reviews. No one will suspect ... until you speak, and your soul *falls out of your mouth like a can of corn from a shelf.* (William Gass, *Habitation of the Word*)

FULL-BRAIN STYLE

For further examples see previous passages under "Smoothing the Flow" by Johnston, Francis, Anderson, Farber and Patterson, Shakespeare, Mailer, Faulkner, Editors of *Sunset Magazine,* Walcott, and Becker. There are also examples under "Giving Pause" by Pruden, Heller, Coover, editors of Apple IIc, editors of Ortho horticulture series, Momaday, Mumford, Agee, and Shakespeare. Many of the melted-together words from Chapter 3 qualify as metaphors.

5
MAKING FACES
Ways to avoid insincerity and intimidation

It is just as important to learn what not do to in writing as it is to learn what to do. One thing a good writer learns not to do is to write when his or her motives for writing are either to inflate the importance of reality or to hide the truth. Aside from usually being immoral or unethical, this inflation and deception is sure to bore at best, and embarrass at worst. This is because smoothing-the-flow, giving-pause, and fine-tuning with metaphor are all principles that stick in the throat when one tries to write inflated or insincere language. These principles are designed to define truth, and they break down or seem ridiculous when they are not used for that purpose.

FULL-BRAIN STYLE

Some writers make a living by writing inflated or insincere prose. These writers can clog the best graduate schools, ladder-climb in the most sophisticated attorney and lawmakers' offices, or collect back-pat at the classiest business correspondence desks. The best way to recognize these writers, to understand how they are manipulating language in negative ways, is by making their face and getting behind their mask. Besides, all of us have known desperate times when we have been tempted to inflate language or hide the truth through twisted prose. Making faces is a way to get this kind of writing out of our systems.

Three different faces to try on are facial packs, attempts to make reality more pleasing than it really is; war paint, attempts to make reality more intimidating than it should be; and metal mask, attempts to make reality more official than it needs to be. In some ways all these faces have to do with euphemism, the substitution of an agreeable or inoffensive word or expression for one that is offensive because it is unpleasant, painful, indelicate, frightful, or embarrassingly trivial and mundane.

FACIAL PACKS

Facial packs are the least objectionable faces to make. These include attempts to make most unimportant, normal-but-unappetizing realities more pleasing than they really are. For instance, no one really cares to go into detail about what pours out of their intestines or where it gets poured. That place was once euphemized as the "toilet," because a toilet was where one merely used cosmetics or shaved. However what happened with "toilet," happens with all euphemisms that are used over a long period of time: the graphic reality, in this case the opening up the intestines, became vivid again, attaching itself to the word "toilet." It was time to cleanse reality with a new facial pack.

The new euphemism for "toilet," simply became a spin-off of another nearby device, the bath. The word "bathroom" still works fairly well as a way to make reality more pleasing, but for some the visual and olfactory realities began to seep in again.

For them the new facial pack involves terms like "little girls' room," "men's room," "lavatory," "powder room," "rest room," "cloak room," "john," "convenience," or "water closet." Sometimes poorly-tuned, bizarre metaphors are used such as "going to make a phone call."

Sex is another area of life that most feel needs masking. For instance, "making love" is a euphemism that covers a wide range of sexual activity from the most innocent, to what some might consider to be the most perverse. On the low end, a woman meets a man in a bar; they talk for twenty minutes; they go out to his car. Once inside, they remove some of their clothes, they insert his genital into hers, and after the man and woman spend a few more hours together, they part, never seeing each other again. When the woman calls a girlfriend later she tells her that she "made love" to this man she just met. To say "insert his genital into hers" realistically depicts the mechanical, loveless act that happened between the man and woman; however, most would prefer a facial pack such as "sexual intercourse." In fact, Latin- or Greek-stemmed words, such as "intercourse," are so antiseptic, softening reality into something so important sounding, that if two people who love each other "fuck" instead of having "intercourse," an offended reader will not only discredit love as a motive for that sexual act, but will probably slam the book shut. If two people who do not love each other, like the two above, "have sexual intercourse," the reader will not only read on, but momentarily consider love as the motive for sex.

Sex films are euphemised as "frank," "unexpurgated," "adult films," appealing to "warm imaginations," "French interests," or "friendly relationships." As with other facials, euphemisms for sex melt away as reality becomes attached to the masking word or phrase, and then new euphemisms must be invented. Of course, social mores play a large part in deciding which realities should be smeared over. During the late 1800's the word leg was considered too meaty and had to be euphemized as "a limb." Most sexual euphemisms serve romantic idealism and only when they help someone pretend they are sexually involved in a way that they really are not, do those euphemisms become dangerous cleansers.

FULL-BRAIN STYLE

Facial pack euphemisms are also used on the names given to jobs and professions. This is an attempt to make those endeavors sound more important or more worthwhile than they really are, and only when they actually prevent someone in the profession, or someone using the profession, from knowing serious truths, are the unreal faces harmful. Otherwise these euphemisms groom harmless self-esteem. For instance, hairdressers changed their name to beauticians; then to stylists; then to cosmetologists. Of course, some of their functions changed during this time too. People who stuffed dead bodies with chemicals, boxed them, and lowered them into a hole in the ground, took on a face called "undertaker" until people really saw themselves being taken under and then undertakers changed their face to "mortician." Electrical contractors, rat killers, and garbage collectors have facial packs such as "electrical engineers," "exterminating engineers," and "sanitation engineers." The titles "assistant manager," "manager," and "executive" are applied to many positions that in reality carry out lesser functions than the name implies.

Products receive the same covering. Used cars masquerade as "repossessed," "rebuilt," or "previously owned." The fifteenth street of a housing tract, on flat land, with no views, and little landscaping, freshens up with a name like "Maple View Lane." A vomit bag on an airplane takes on a friendlier face if it is labeled "for motion discomfort." Some stores will not carry a "small" jock strap or athletic support, only "medium," "large," or "extra large." The pentagon can inflate a budget for toothpicks if they are called "wood interdental stimulators."

Some facial packs really depend on what side of the pack someone is on as to whether reality is being hoodwinked. For instance, several years ago sports columnist Jim Murray pointed out the football team we favor is "poised," "confident," and "shows class," but if the other team possesses the same attributes they are "over-confident," "conceited," and "arrogant." Our quarterback plays "mistake-free football," but theirs is a "robot;" our team is "hard-hitting" but their players are "cheap-shot artists;" and our team "gets upset because they hate to lose," but theirs does because they are "a bunch of crybabies." Likewise at the work place, it depends on one's insight into reality as to whether another should be considered "experienced" or "over the hill." Reality says that one of those references is merely a facial pack. Is an office or department "wracked with dissension," or does it have a "healthy difference of opinion;" is its leadership "compassionate" or "weak;" are the people that work there "dedicated" or "psychotic;" do the workers "bargain" or "demand;" do people have "friends" or "cronies;" is there a "governing force" or a "ruling clique?" These distinctions are more important than the football ones. Distinguishing which word or phrase here is the facial pack, and which one is reality, can become very important in deciding on political, professional, moral, and ethical issues.

WORK OUT

The best way to dramatize the ability of facial packs to clean up reality, is to take any mundane, normal-but-unappealing, or other avoided reality such as those discussed above, and describe it without using any abstract words or phrases, including ones that are medical, philosophical, scientific, or social-scientific. Describe the reality in step by step detail with a matter-of-fact tone, and in as literal language as possible. If you are describing an activity or process, include the details at the beginning of the action and move to the last details of the action. If you are describing an item, describe it in detail and explain exactly what it does or is used for. Do not spare the reader anything, including what you know the reader does not want to hear. This part of the assignment will usually take about a half a typed page.

Following the description, list five original euphemisms or facial packs, each of which could replace the entire process or procedure you described realistically. Remember that euphemism does not include well-tuned metaphors or innocent language; those devices help make reality as vivid as it really is. Facial packs make reality more pleasing than it really is. Misdirected metaphors, soothing words, and big, scientific-sounding words can lead to original euphemisms. For instance, pretend you are

FULL-BRAIN STYLE

a mortician and know that "untimely release," "eternal rest," and "pass away" have all been used too often to refer to death. Dark, humorous phrases, like "kick the bucket," are anti-euphemistic in the sense that they are not unctious, but still their humor deflates the pain of death and distracts from the grotesqueness of death. You need to come up with five new words or phrases for your staff to use, ranging from darkly humorous to very serious ones, in order to please themselves or customers with different attitudes towards death. All the new terms must help soften the blow of death's reality.

WAR PAINT

Writers put on war paint when they want to sound impressive and intimidate their readers. The paint creates a superficial brilliance, exaggerating the writer's importance. A reader that realizes this is not so easily victimized by writers who wear war paint. These writers have usually pumped themselves up so much in order to get their face prepped that they are unable to see how foolish they appear to a knowing victim. As William Blake says, "He who has suffered you to impose on him knows you."

One of the colors of war paint is the over-use or unnecessary use of "big" words. These are usually the multi-syllabic words in English that have Latin and Greek origins as opposed to Germanic, Anglo-Saxon origins, which are often simpler, one syllable words. The fact that English is made up from both Latin-Greek and German-Anglo-Saxon language bases makes English a rich and exacting language, a language that can differentiate between fine shades of meaning. For instance, "said" is an Anglo-Saxon based word that means something very different from the Latin based word "indicated," that derives from the Latin word for "say" or "speak." In English, "indicated" can imply a response that is either less committed, or less direct, or more vague than "said." In fact, "indicated" can just as easily imply communication through lifted eyebrows as communication through speech.

But someone putting on war paint ignores this difference, writing "indicated" even when he or she means "said." They do this for two reasons: "indicated " sounds more impressive and also, because of the more subtle meanings of "indicated," the writer avoids the responsibility of being sure that something was actually "said." War paint often kills language in more than one way because the two deceptions, one in voice, the other in content, go together. For instance a person who does not really understand what he is writing about or is trying to make something sound more important than reality permits, can perplex a reader with a face full of war paint. That writer makes himself seem superior by using war paint, and at the same time knows that his paint will help camouflage any arguments and facts that might otherwise not seem so intimidating.

A typical example of this would be when a lawyer or business correspondent for an automobile manufacturer has to admit in a recall letter to a customer that the company's poor workmanship might kill the customer. The writer would have to sound intimidating, inflating his or her voice enough to sound beyond reproach, and at the same time flatten the dangerous reality by making it less understandable, so as to quiet the customer's anger and shift the blame away from the manufacturer. War paint does both. The writer might write that a certain "deficiency" could "adversely affect vehicle control." "Deficiency" paints over "poor manufacturing" and "adversely affect vehicle control" paints over "the car could crash, killing you." Some might call the war paint professional writing. It is nothing but distortion. When death is involved, for instance during surgery or in an air crash, "professional" war paint, like "therapeutic misadventure" and "involuntary conversion of a 727 jet," seems grotesque.

Coupled with the over-use and misuse of Latin- and Greek-based words, sheer volume of unnecessary words adds even more muscle to a face of loud colors. Every student has one time or another tried to make up for lack of knowledge with extra lines of words; many teachers have tried to fill unimportant lectures with mouthfuls of file notes; many grant writers have tried to build up mediocre proposals by attaching extra forms of words; many lawmakers have pleased everyone by loading laws with enough language for people on opposite political sides to claim victory. Simplisitic, inconsequential, or even dishonest content already dried with war paint, is made bolder by painting over and over it with the same paint.

For instance, the following is a typical excerpt from the *Congressional Record:* "The oil price structure should give the President a substantial measure of administrative flexibility to craft the price regulatory mechanism in a manner designed to optimize production from domestic properties subject to a statutory parameter requiring the regulatory pattern to prevent prices from exceeding a maximum weighted average." A previous president of the National Council of Teachers of English thought that what this sentence really said was "Congress should authorize the President to design an oil price structure. The system must encourage domestic production but outlaw exorbitant prices."

Most English teachers, like the president of the National Council of Teachers of English, know such writing in the *Congressional Record* is the result of disregard for basic composition principles. But it is also well crafted war paint, an attempt to sound important, yet avoid the responsibility of making a request that might be unpopular.

Aside from blown-up words and wordiness, a fainter hue often applied to war paint is the passive voice. This involves over-use of the verb "to be," and having the subject of a sentence acted upon instead of doing the action. For instance, instead of saying "The apple fell from the tree," a war-painted writer would say "The apple has been separated from the tree," "The apple is known to be off the tree," "The apple was dropped from the tree's branches," or any other construction that uses a "to be" verb to have the apple acted upon instead of doing the action itself. The psychological effect is to make the apple more precious by cushioning it with superfluous words and thinking of it as an object that is beyond exertion. Weakening the verb and inflating the importance of the apple can also be accomplished by proceeding the original sentence with an indefinite it-phrase: "It is known," "It is believed," or "It seems that" placed in front of "the apple fell from the tree." All slightly inflate the apple's reality. The passive voice and it-phrases are subtle war paint hues, but they add just enough color to the nose area so that it lifts slightly higher in the air.

WORK OUT

The moral, ethical, and social implications associated with the problem of making faces with the loud colors of war paint are usually more serious than those associated with facial pack. It is important to understand what it takes to make this face. One of the best ways to get behind a face full of this kind of gobbledygook is to take a common expression, famous quotation, nursery rhyme, or well-known adage, and rewrite it so it speaks from a face full of strange color.

To do this, take simple words and make them more complicated. Take simple actions or items and break them into smaller unnecessary parts, and use more words than are necessary. So, "The grass is always greener on the other side of the fence," becomes "The growth of minute, macilent leaves consistently and invariably exists in a more stimulating propagation, and in a higher realm of verdant hue or vibrant chlorophyll on the territory and confines antipodal to the separating barrier that is hued from heavily vegetated terrain and then fabricated for use of property definiton." And a nursery rhyme like "Mary had a little lamb as white as snow. Everywhere that Mary went the lamb was sure to go," becomes "It is known that a young female homo sapien had sole proprietorship of a small, docile quadruped with a pelt that was reminiscent of precipitation in the form of small white ice crystals. Regardless of how far and wide said female did perambulate, and whatever location she did happen upon, the small docile quadruped was there concomitant."

METAL MASK

As discussed in chapter four, metaphoric slang is often a lively expression of truth, but jargon, official labels, and buzz words, are not. Instead of making language more lively or reality more accurate, jargon sterilizes life by simplifying it, protecting the reader from something complex that deserves more thought or explanation. A writer who becomes fascinated with jargon wears a metal mask, cutting himself or herself off from the reader and cutting the reader off from reality.

A writer with metal mask is usually more chilling than one with facial pack, since the metal-masked writer simplifies complex, important-to-understand realities, as opposed to cleaning up simple ones. In a way, metal mask is a colder, more efficient version of war paint. It condenses all the twisted and tangled language of war paint into official terminology, and official terminology has a thought-through, mesmerizing reserve that seems less penetrable than war paint.

All professional, governmental, and academic endeavors have their own hypnotic language chanted by their own expert metal maskers. For instance there are people who live in cardboard houses or demolished buildings; whose schools are a mess and whose English is almost unrecognizable; who are resentful of people who have money and know they have little chance of ever making substantial amounts of money themselves, unless they do it illegally through murder, robbery, or drug sales; or if satisfied with meager income, obtain it by doing menial, back-breaking work; and who are treated as less than human because of the pigment in their skin. Metal mask protects a sociologist or government official from mentioning, and eventually, from even thinking about, these details. It sedates the pain of these details through a single, official, neutral-sounding word or phrase: "disadvantaged," "underprivileged," "occupiers of substandard housing," or "culturally deprived."

Metal maskers argue that such jargon-face is necessary: it is a code for complex problems and so makes discussion of problems simpler and quicker. But sometimes metal mask can unintentionally hide reality from innocent students in a sociology or political science class; at worst, it can hide reality from government budget committees or private assistance groups that could help change the people's living conditions. The more students, professors, and officials economize with this jargon, the more they psychologically deep freeze the very reality they were initially so concerned about.

The grotesque, frightening realities of nuclear power accidents and other pollution messes get their own unique disguises. For instance, the nuclear power industry has referred to explosions and other nuclear reactor accidents as "energetic disassemblies," "rapid oxidations," "plant transients," and "plutonium taking up residence." Only someone who can take himself or herself so seriously and worry so much about selfprotection, can hide such dangerous reality from others by putting on such a psychologically stiff face. Metal masks are not always so elaborate, nor do they always rely solely on Latin-based words. Sometimes official jargon is seductively simple. For instance, many years ago a Colorado state legislator, A.J. Spano, tried to hide the fact that Denver's air was the second-dirtiest in the nation by changing the words on the air-quality scale: "hazardous" would be changed to "poor," "dangerous" to "acceptable," "very unhealthful" to "fair," "unhealthful" to "good," and "moderate" to "very good."

George Orwell was one of the first to pull the disguise off jargon used to mask military atrocities. During the wars of this century, waged by different countries with different ideologies, the same jargon, or close versions of it, has continued to serve those who need to cushion war's horrors. For instance, when small, defenseless towns and villages have been bombarded from the air, inhabitants driven from their homes, livestock machine-gunned, grain supplies torched, women raped, and civilians massacred, a metal masker will call this "neutralization" or "pacification." Taking over countries might be called an "incursion" or "rectification of frontiers," and killing people, without a trial, who are suspected of either having sympathy with the enemy or who are used as scapegoats to build unification through hate, is called "elimination of unreliable elements" or to "terminate with extreme prejudice." It is easier to kill and allow killing when protected by metal mask.

FULL-BRAIN STYLE 67

One reason metal mask neuters reality is because, like war paint, it usually relies on abstract language that in itself has vague, general implications at best, and almost no meaning at worst. This fact is best dramatized by the Systematic Buzz Phrase Projector. A number of years ago, with aptly obscure origins, although some credit the inner workings of the Royal Canadian Air Force, the Systematic Buzz Phrase Projector came into being. Later a U.S. Public Health Service official circulated and popularized it. By mixing three words at random from three columns of high-tech-sounding words, one could invent computer age terminology that meant nothing at all, but to the insecure ear, sounded as if it meant something of utmost importance. The following is a partial list of the three columns from the Phrase Projector:

	A	B	C
0	Integrated	Management	Options
1	Total	Organizational	Flexibility
2	Systemized	Monitored	Capability
3	Parallel	Reciprocal	Mobility

The phrases seem impressive enough read straight across, but when an audience begins to find out the phrases are meaningless or easy covers for something more ambiguous and beyond a pin down, then the bureaucrat in charge needs only to jump around at random between the different columns. Who would dare question the validity of the following: "Integrated Organizational Capability," "Systemized Management Options," "Total Monitored Mobility"?

It is easy for some humanists and artists to decry the bureaucrats, politicians, and social scientists who so easily slip on metal mask, but they can do it too, and with great expertise and smoothness. Sometimes art history, theology, film, music, and architecture professors and critics erase the complexities of great works of art with one glossy word: "neo-classic," "existential," "Jacobean," "neo-realistic," "baroque," "surrealistic," "post-modern," "abstract expressionistic," "neosurrealistic," and so on. It is possible to sit through an entire art history lecture, watching a professor flash fifty slides while validating the worth of every one with the word "baroque," as if the word were a magic wand, and never realize that each painting is a special expression either having a unique sense of humor, or capturing a psychological state of mind in a way never attempted before, or expressing a complex point of view on a moral issue through subtle use of composition, or using color and light to give an important historical or mythical event timeless implications.

Some literary critics and English teachers are as guilty of metal mask as anyone in the humanities. The same English teacher that tells writing classes that jargon blemishes the faces of politicians and bureaucrats, might stride across the hall the next period to teach a literature class, tingling to set an example for students who enjoy verbal jousting. This teacher forgets that this jousting will be at the expense of truly learning to love literature. These tournaments flow with such weapon phrases as "semiotic discourses," "symbolic registers," "formalistic breakdowns," "psycholinguistic truths," "Oedipal yearnings," "experimental anti-myths," "very derivative of _____ (fill in with any great author's or philosopher's name)," or "heightened _____ (fill in with "reality," "tragedy," "language," or just about any other word having to do with literature). Sometimes a student can listen to a whole lecture on a book, or even go through a whole semester of a literature course, with his or her mind buzzing with catch words, never hearing a professor point out an author's subtle sense of humor, relate a book's moral sensibility to problems that interest students, or mention interesting facets of a fictional character's behavior and thoughts.

The murder of great art is not as horrifying as the murder of people, but it is still painful.

WORK OUT

The best thing about metal mask is that it is easy to parody. J. Robertson and G. Osborne once made fun of jargon or official language in mock directions for *Datamation Magazine* entitled "Postal System Input Buffer Device." The title itself is

FULL-BRAIN STYLE

made-up jargon for a mailbox. In order to be able to build up a large list of jargon for operating this device, they first constructed an involved outline of directions, breaking the simple task of dropping letters into a mailbox into several pages of numbered, paragraphed procedures, including "Position of Operator," "Initial Setup," "Start Operations," "Feed Cycles;" sprinkled these steps with parenthetical "notes" and "warnings;" then crammed original jargon into every line of the directive. For instance, the handle on the mailbox was called a "Multifunction Control Lever," "But Gate" was the name given to the door of the opening, "one full Operation Cycle" had to do with dropping one letter into the box, referred to as a "box memory."

Speak through metal mask by doing what Robertson and Osborne did: take a simple procedure such as washing the face or throwing out the garbage or putting on clothes or kissing; break it into a least six steps sprinkled with notes and warnings; and label the steps and as many other items as possible with your own creative metal-masked terms and phrases. A thesaurus can be of great help in developing your inventions. Once you practice metal mask, realizing how easily it can make anything inaccessible through official-sounding prattle, there is a chance that it will then seem laughable to depend on jargon when writing about more serious issues.

PART II
FULL-BLOODED STRATEGY

1
PUTTING TOGETHER HUMPTY-DUMPTY
Introduction to Full-Blooded Strategy

Full-Blooded Strategy is a collection of writing pursuits built on professional writing examples. By working through the pursuits, you will discover that designing and building an entire written piece, for any occasion, can be creative and stimulating.

The notion that an ideal organization or strategy for writing exists is an illusion shattered by all learning-to-write books. Beginning with the ancient Greek philosopher, Aristotle, works on writing strategy knock the written world off the wall, and then collect different written works back together again under types and categories, making various writing tactics easier for student writers to perceive. But Aristotle probably never intended his categories to be cast in bronze: he did not create his categories out of god-given visions, but derived them through careful observation of successful speakers of his day. If still alive, he would have taken another look, creating new classifications that take into account writing successes since his days in ancient Greece.

However, collecting writing strategies into groups, even new ones, runs the risk of ossifying writing into separate, stony blocks, giving writers the false impression that different types of writing never intertwine or temper each other, when in fact they do more often than they do not. Full-Blooded Strategy knocks the written world off the wall too, but here all the king's horses and all the king's men do not worry too much about putting that world totally back together again. Here the written world is one of infinite possibilities. Instead of being labeled by categories, the strategies are titled to reflect the intriguing aspects of the exemplary models, and subtitled to suggest their broad applicability.

Furthermore, when Full-Blooded Strategy knocks the written world off the wall, individual written works are left broken open a bit for careful scrutiny of their insides. This allows for upfront, focused analysis of the strengths of written pieces so that you can move quickly to work outs to test that particular strategy's strengths.

With the exception of the last chapter, enjoy picking chapters that seem the most intriguing and doing these first. Some chapters may seem more complex or more academic than others, but no chapter here is more important than any other. None demand less imagination or less rationality than another. You should not try to do more than one chapter a week since each one demands intense thought and must be absorbed over time. Also, an essential part of creativity is in being so involved in your work that you enjoy constantly going back over it to rethink, revise, and polish what you have written. All good writers know that it is impossible to refine the ideas in a written piece until something is down on paper (or up on a monitor) to work on. That means you will make at least one revision. And then you will need to revise the work at least once again, giving extra attention to full-brain style.

2
RAISING THE DEAD
Resurrecting past ideas

One powerful way to discuss historical or philosophical change is to have a fictitious persona from the past suddenly reappear and confront the present with the writer serving as tour guide. For instance, imagine the shock of a pilot from World War II or the Viet Nam War, missing in action when he was twenty years old, if he were to appear today, now over sixty years old or over forty years old. What would he think about his family, American values, or the political scene? He has never heard of super bowls, fast food institutions, or MTV.

In Fyodor Dostoyevsky's *The Brothers Karamazov,* one of the

FULL-BLOODED STRATEGY

most famous Russian novels of the 1800's and of all time, Ivan tells his brother Alyosha of imagining Jesus to return and appear in Spain during the Grand Inquisition only to be told by the Grand Inquisitor that He has no right to add anything to what He said of old. But what if Jesus did have that right, and what if He appeared today? What would shock Him most? Would He have anything to add about bumper stickers, a certain television envangelist, ceremonies conducted by the Pope, a suburban Presbyterian church, old barns in the South with "Jesus Saves" scrawled over them? And what mundane thing would catch his attention that most of us would not have expected Him to notice?

If you were a tour guide for Jesus or any other spiritually or historically famous guest from the past, how would you as host go about explaining what the guest saw? Would the guest's insights come into sharper focus and make more of an impression on your reader if you played a naive tour guide and responded with innocent shock to your guest's observations? Or could you stoke more passion from this guest by playing the devil's advocate, dismissing or arguing against your guest's concerns? Or perhaps it would be better for you to lighten the guest's shock of the present and also amuse the reader by being a witty or humorous host?

WORK OUT

Have someone from the past reappear and confront the present with his or her past. You could have a rock star, such as Buddy Holly, reappear and be introduced to today's music. But first you may want to have him or her listen to missed, interim rock music: The Beatles, The Beach Boys, Simon and Garfunkel, Blondie, Elvis Costello, Cyndi Lauper, Michael Jackson and more until you reach the present. You could have a sports figure, such as Babe Ruth, watch his sport today. Maybe have Einstein review new technology since his death: nuclear weapons, nuclear energy, "the chip," or space shuttles. The possibilities are endless. You may even decide to deal with more intimate historical changes and have a dead family member, real or imaginary, return and review what has happened to your family.

The essential element is to write about a subject with which you are knowledgeable. You must be familiar with historical realities or the written piece will go flat. Also crucial is that you make a clear decision on what your attitude or role as tour guide will be. One other item will enrich your piece. If past written dialogue or published books by the guest exist, try to imitate their writing or speaking style.

3
SPLITTING THE SECOND
Detailing momentary realities

The following paragraph from *House Made of Dawn* by the famous American Indian writer, Natachee Scott Momady, is an description of two eagles maneuvering through mating rites that leaves the reader in a state of awe:

"They were golden eagles, a male and a female, in their mating flight. They were cavorting, spinning and spiraling on the cold, clear columns of air, and they were beautiful. They swooped and hovered, leaning on the air, and swung close together, feinting and screaming with delight. The female was fullgrown, and the span of her broad wings was greater than any man's height.

There was a fine flourish to her motion; she was deceptively, incredibly fast, and her pivots and wheels were wide and full-bloom. But her great weight was streamlined and perfectly controlled. She carried a rattlesnake; it hung shining from her feet, limp and curving out in the trail of her flight. Suddenly her wings and tail fanned, catching full on the wind, and for an instant she was still, widespread and spectral in the blue, while her mate flared past and away, turning around in the distance to look for her. Then she began to beat upward at an angle from the rim until she was small in the sky, and she let go of the snake. It fell slowly, writhing and rolling, floating out like a bit of silver thread against the wide backdrop of the land. She held still above, buoyed up on the cold current, her crop and hackles gleaming like copper in the sun. The male swerved and sailed. He was younger than she and a little more than half as large. He was quicker, tighter in his moves. He let the carrion drift by; then suddenly he gathered himself and stooped, sliding down in a blur of motion to the strike. He hit the snake on the head, with not the slightest deflection of his course or speed, cracking its long body like a whip. Then he rolled and swung upward in a great pendulum arc, riding out his momentum. At the top of his glide he let go of the snake in turn, but the female did not go for it. Instead she soared out over the plain, nearly out of sight, like a mote receding into the haze of the far mountain. The male followed, and Abel watched them go, straining to see, saw them veer once, dip and disappear."

This piece provides a perfect example of the way time can be suspended in written description. Although the action described happens within seconds, the experience is so filled out with descriptive detail that it takes much longer to read and savour the experience than the actual event could have covered in real time. The writer could have used lightening description that would have approximated the speed of the event: "The eagles mating was an awesome experience." But an all-encompassing, sweeping word like "awesome" sucks up all the details that prove that the experience was awesome. In fact, as readers we never feel that Momaday is cheating with reality. On the contrary, we can only feel that reality is being made more vivid, and that we

FULL-BLOODED STRATEGY

are seeing details that would have been missed if we had witnessed the actual event.

To do this kind of writing, Momaday had to perceive the action in slow motion, his mind breaking the action into separate, smaller parts. It is as if Momaday had become a physicist's strobe light, "stopping the action down." Once each quick action is slowed down and broken into parts, each part can undergo careful observation and description, applying all the rules of full-brain grammar. All good writers learn to slow action and events down in order build those realities into a piece of writing.

WORK OUT

Pick out a walking course that can be traveled within ten to twenty seconds. Walking through this space you would normally move too quickly to notice or even care about details and subtle changes. Now put the walk into slow motion by breaking this area into three smaller spaces, perhaps ten to twenty square feet per area. Ideally, one area should contain something dramatic like a multi-trunk tree or an interesting stairway; another area should be very mundane, like an expanse of cement or carpeting.

Force yourself to spend at least thirty minutes taking notes on each area, until you have pushed out two to three pages of notes. This will force you to look closely and not take anything for granted, unlike most viewers of fast movements who take most details for granted while being overwhelmed by the swiftness of the action. Take notes on everything: stains, light reflections, sounds, changes in grass structure, insects, textures, and colors. Stay away from abstract words such as beautiful, ugly, and dirty. If something is beautiful, describe it so the reader will believe it without your telling that it is. If something is amusing, describe it with details that make it amusing.

After taking notes for almost two hours, you are ready to describe a walk that in reality takes place within the quickness of seconds. Rewrite your notes into a two page typewritten paper. The reader should feel that the writer or narrator is moving through three well defined spaces, one following the next in a linear sequence. Decide what overall mood such as depression, ecstasy, paranoia, or awe, best unifies the whole description. Deciding this will help you determine which details to keep, which ones deserve slight exaggeration, which ones seemed important at the time but now need to be played down or left out. You should never allude to feelings or thoughts; let the full-blown description itself convey what this twenty second walk means to the narrator, just as the awe and excitement felt by Momaday's persona is never directly referred to. Realities made of details often speak more powerfully than abstract or judgemental statements.

4
MOCKING WITH MASS MEDIA
Deflating media or mentalities

One way to satirize the cliches of a particular group's mentality is to objectify it through an outlandish event that in turn is subjected to the cliches of a news media format. The advantage of this set-up is that the details of the event and the cliches of the news format both end up magnifying each other, rendering each other ridiculous. For instance, the following excerpts are from a mock newspaper article entitled "God Is Dead in Georgia" written by Anthony Towne. Towne has two targets: a formulaic newspaper style and people who see God in materialistic or political terms.

WRITEFUL

ATLANTA, GA, Nov. 9 — God, creator of the universe, principal diety of the world's Jews, ultimate reality of Christians, and most eminent of all divinities, died late yesterday during major surgery undertaken to correct a massive diminishing influence.

. . .

Assisting Dr. Altizer in the unsuccessful surgery were Dr. Paul van Buren of Temple University, Philadelphia; Dr. William Hamilton of Colgate-Rochester, Rochester, N.Y.; and Dr. Gabriel Vahanian of Syracuse University, Syracuse N.Y.

. . .

...the Pope, in Rome, said, in part: "We are deeply distressed for we have suffered an incalculable loss. The contributions of God to the Church cannot be measured, and it is difficult to imagine how we shall proceed without Him."

. . .

(In New York, meanwhile, the stock market dropped sharply in early trading. Volume was heavy ... The market rallied in late trading, after reports were received that Jesus —- see 'Man in the News,' p.36, col.4—who survives, plans to assume a larger role in the management of the universe.)

. . .

"At least he's out of his misery," commented one housewife in an Elmira, N.Y. supermarket.

. . .

(There have been unconfirmed reports that Jesus of Nazareth, 33, a carpenter and reputed son of God, who survives will assume the authority, if not the title, of the deceased diety. Jesus, sometimes called the Christ, was himself a victim of death, having succumbed some 1932 years ago ... The case is complicated by the fact that Jesus, although he died, returned to life, and so may not have died at all...)

. . .

(Next Sunday's New York Times will include, without extra charge, a 24-page full-color supplement with many photographs, reviewing the major events of God's long reign ... The editors will be grateful for pertinent letters, photographs, visions and the like.)

FULL-BLOODED STRATEGY 83

Each of the excerpts provides an example of the typical, formulaic devices used in many newspaper articles: the sqeezing of as many credentials as possible into a railroad-ramble sentence; the inclusion of trivial details with what are at best, secondary people involved in the incident; the focus on the most cliche but official responses; the diversion of attending to other parts of the newspaper; the focus on cliches from man-on-the-street people; the careful concern to avoid controversy by using safe words such as "unconfirmed," "reputed," "if not," "sometimes," "the case is complicated by the fact," and other words or phrases that make it clear that the newspaper is covering its legal and political flanks; and allusion to "human interest" stories in order to turn intimate or complex details into souvenir shop items.

Television newsreporting has its own formulaic devices. For instance, an early format was, and still is, the weather report with its over concern with unimportant details such as temperatures in cities most of us could not care less about. In the 1980's television added new special reporters to lift our eyelids over details we never thought much about before: grocery experts to remind us that we are not cutting our pineapples correctly; auto reporters to remind us to check for oil leaks in places that we will never remember; and consumer reporters to boil our rage over an ice cream cone manufacturer's claims that he puts less sugar in the cones than he really does.

The old "Saturday Night Live" satires included Gilda Ratner who mocked this special-concern reporter through her character Rosanne Rosanna Danna. She was a wild special assignment reporter who would work up a sweat over anything, no matter how trivial, and end up on something even more trivial about that thing, usually its unimaginably minute or grotesque aspect. There are many other formats, phrases, and motifs in television news broadcasting that become standard, and are used indiscriminately, regardless of the subject or essence of a story.

WORK OUT
Study the newspaper techniques listed above, or watch television news shows and list their typical words, phrases, and for-

mats. Then use one medium or another to write about a subject. (If you write a TV news script, you may need to do several short news items dealing with different related issues.) It is essential your subject be extraordinary either in the sense that it is too important to be reduced to a news item, or too trivial to deserve a news story. The newspaper article above provides an example of a subject too important. Other possibilities might include stories that scientists have just learned the sun will burn out tomorrow, Socrates will return to Greece next week, or men and women will no longer be allowed to see one another. Trivial stories might include one on John Smith who has finally learned to tie his shoes. Be careful. Some stories that seem trivial enough for this work out, such as a fast food chain deciding to fold its tacos differently, would actually get a news story; so some trivial topics might not work as well as others.

5
ANIMAL TALK
Capturing zoological details

Book and documentary film writers who describe and define animals, often clip the wings of their own human innocence and excitement in fear of losing their "scientific objectivity." In extreme cases, this self-clip manifests itself in identification manuals filled with flat prose that is marked by incomplete sentences and pruned language. The psychological, if not overt, assumption made by these writers is that this language is "objective" because it has the terseness of mathematics, as opposed to the elaboration of the subjective mind. The other assumption is that all details, to be treated objectively, should be treated with equal importance, one blending into the other.

A case in point is the Roger Peterson bird-manual description of a bird that "runs on the ground (tracks show 2 toes forward, 2 aft). Large, slender, streaked; with a long white-tipped tail, shaggy crest, strong legs. White crescent on open wing." The writer also flattens out the bird's range, voice ("Song, 6-8 dovelike coo's descending in pitch ..."), and, in some editions, even the food.

There is one main problem with this clipped "objective description": it would not help anyone who was struggling in the field to see and positively identify this bird for the first time. The reader would have field trouble because so many of the bird's characteristics are shared with other birds, and the writer is not doing anything to help the reader absorb the uniqueness of this bird's particular combination of such details. The reader simply sinks into a swamp full of information bits.

One way to help the reader is for the writer to isolate the most dominant, eye-catching details of the bird, regardless of what category those details belong to, so they are not lost in the mud. One pleasant way to frame those details is with a riddle format: short sentences in third person singular (he, she, it), holding off on the animal or bird's name until the end of the list of the predominant details. By holding off on the "answer," the details attain a life of their own that press firmly into the reader's mind, which is still attentive, uncluttered by the self-satisfaction of knowing the animal's name.

This is how another bird writer, George Hollister, starts his description of the same bird identified above: "He's half tail and half feet. The rest of him is head and beak. When he runs, he moves on blurring wheels. He can turn on a dime and leave change. He doesn't need to fly because he can run faster. He kicks dirt in a snake's face, and then eats the snake." What is he? Finally we are told: he's the roadrunner. Some might argue that a statement such as "he's half tail and half feet" is not objective. But seen in a flash, this is what the roadrunner really is, it is all he is, and knowing just that one truth, someone in the field could identify this bird when another person who has read pages of bland information bits, could not.

FULL-BLOODED STRATEGY 87

Someone else might also complain that metaphors are non-objective; the reader of this book knows otherwise. That other, self-clipped person might also complain about Hollister's long sentences later in the description: "He dashes in circles around a coiled snake, stops within striking distance, shuffles his feet, swishes his tail in the dirt and stirs up a blinding cloud of dust." But this railroad ramble helps to capture reality, smoothing the flow of interrelated actions.

Hollister uses another device that helps give material more importance, incubating it for easy remembrance in the field or even for a zoology exam. Most zoology texts, animal encyclopedias, and animal identification manuals will mention interesting or amazing abilities the animal has, such as bizarre mating maneuvers, impossible feeding habits, or genius engineering feats of survival, before dramatizing, if mentioning at all, the problem the animal overcomes by its unique ability. These writers take such details for granted, no longer astonished by what they know. Hollister does the opposite; he knows if the reader is momentarily involved in a seemingly impossible problem first, then he will look more intensely for the solution, for the detail that makes the animal unique, and usually more capable than humans.

For instance, Hollister first describes, with threatening details, the roadrunner's hot environment and hyper-activity that would both seem to dehydrate the bird, and only then, the reader's mouth becoming drier with every word, does the writer mention the roadrunner's ability to locate shade and feed on reptiles of high water content. In another problem, the writer emphasizes the long length of a snake dinner, pointing out that it takes as much talent to eat something longer than the roadrunner as it does to catch it. Only then does he mention the bird's superactive digestive juices that slowly burn off the head-swallowed-first meal. Other writers would simply list details like eating high water content animals and burning them off with digestive juices, never allowing the reader to absorb the reality these abilities overcome.

Descriptions of animals can be both fun and objective. One of the quickest ways to endanger the life of an animal is to eye it as chopped, standardized bits, sterilized for an information stew.

WORK OUT

Go to the library and look up information on a mammal, insect, bird, reptile or other animal. Rewrite the material using full-brain grammar throughout. Start the writing with a riddle-like paragraph: short sentences starting with third person plural, that introduce the animal's most predominant details; then ending the paragraph with the name of the animal. Dramatize the problems the animal must overcome in eating, mating, fighting, and other aspects of living, before telling how the animal solves the problem.

Dramatizing problems may take some more research since the information you are looking at may take the problems for granted, not giving you the details you need. In his essay, "On Being the Right Size," from his book, *Possible Worlds and other Papers,* J.B.S. Haldane, a world authority on heredity, provides general material on the way different sizes and shapes solve problems for all animals. For instance, he points out that gravity is no problem for a mouse who is thrown down a thousand-yard mine shaft, but in the same situation, the weight of a rat would be enough to kill it; a man would be broken; a horse would "splash." However the film of water on our bodies, something we think nothing of carrying from a bath since it weighs roughly a pound, is more than a burden to a mouse. It could sink it. And even the normal film of water carried on a dunked mouse is a burden since it's equal to the mouse's own weight.

Often you can simply imagine the problem a human would have in dealing with the animal's situation. For instance, it does not take much imagination to dramatically detail the problems a black widow and preying mantis male have if they can be killed by their female counterparts during mating.

Be sure to give credit to the authors and books you take your primary information from, even though you are rewriting their material.

6
NICE GIANTS
Sketching positive achievements

A gripping way to write biographical sketches that are truthful in spirit is to exaggerate people's special attributes, momentarily turning the people into god-like giants. The syndicated sports columnist, Jim Murray, and the social and fictional writer, Norman Mailer, are pros at this kind of mythologizing. Two articles written by Murray, "Bubba—He's Just About the Biggest Pussycat Ever" regarding the great pro football lineman Bubba Smith, and Murray's "These Guys Are Double and Trouble" about the two hotshot basketball pros Ralph Sampson and Akeem Olajuwon, along with Mailer's opening chapter on the famous movie star Marilyn Monroe in *Marilyn, A Biography,* provide typical

FULL-BLOODED STRATEGY

ways to build nice giants. The sports articles are mostly humorous in tone; the chapter on Marilyn is more serious, but both writers write with affection in dramatizing the truthful essence of their subjects.

One device both writers use is to compare their charmers to famous names in other fields. For instance, Murray points out that, in "the little world of football, the name *Bubba* invokes the same kind of terror *Geronimo* did in the old West, or *Attila* in pre-medieval Europe, or *Capone* in prohibition Chicago." Mailer uses metaphor in referring to the world renowned violin maker, saying that "Marilyn was deliverance, a very Stradivarius of sex, so gorgeous, forgiving, humorous, compliant and tender that even the most mediocre musician would relax his lack of art in the dissolving magic of her violin."

A second way to erect a nice giant is to discuss the person as if she or he were a geographical phenomenon, one that competes with the natural elements. Bubba is "a name that has gone into the language to symbolize a creature so awesome that if you saw it swimming ashore in New York Harbor, you'd evacuate the city," and "was one of the scenic wonders of North America." In regard to Olajuwon and Sampson, who look like "double jeopardy to most observers," Murray adds that it's like being "hit with flood and blizzard at the same time. Death and Taxes. Famine and Pestilence." On the other hand, Marilyn, who preferred "those wandering lights on the screen when the luminous life of her face grew ten feet tall," spans all geographical space: "Across five continents the men who knew the most about love would covet her, and the classical pimples of the adolescent working his first gas pump would also pump for her..."

Most important, giants perform feats that would rival both the best in the animal kingdom and the best in the kingdom of gods. With Bubba, "no one had ever seen anything this big and this fast outside of a cage before. Civilians crossed the street when they saw him coming. When he hit the pros he "began tossing quarterbacks around like confetti." In the basketball article, Murray points to "that old bromide of how, if it hadn't been for a clerical error or a sloppy scouting report, Willie Mays, Henry Aaron, and Roberto Clemente might have wound up in the same outfield ... horror-story stuff because, had it happened, baseball, as we know it, might have disappeared." Likewise Sampson and Olajuwon may become "The Creatures That Ate Basketball." Mailer reminds us that Marilyn "was our angel, the sweet angel of sex," and "she gave the feeling that if you made love to her, why then how could you not move more easily into sweets and the purchase of the full promise of future sweets, move into tender heavens where your flesh would be restored."

One minor detail. When one talks to giants, one must be tactful. This adds a bit of cartoonishness to a nice giant profile, fitting only to the sports articles here. Bubba thinks his greatest defeat by Joe Namath's Jets was probably a fix. Murray says, "If you think Bubba is wrong in this, *you* tell him." With the basketball giants, "you can imagine the delicacy with which management had to ask Sampson if he'd mind, heh-heh, just moving over a step or two to make way for this, ah, er, well, less-experienced ... young Nigerian."

The most interesting thing to notice with nice giants, is the way they are not giants at all, but more human than human. Bubba was "the world's biggest collection of fudge. Without his helmet on, Bubba Smith was just a big pussycat of a man who wanted nothing more than to be loved. It pained him when people blanched at introduction or hastily began looking around for the exits." Sampson glares and bites his tongue, staying cool with terse, literal responses as he answers insulting, prying questions by nosy reporters. Marilyn dissolves into one of our more simplistic selves: "In her ambition, so Faustian, and in her ignorance of culture's dimensions, in her liberation and her tyrannical desires, her noble democratic longings intimately contradicted by the widening pool of narcissism (where every friend and slave must bathe), we can see the magnified mirror of ourselves ... "

WORK OUT
Write about a well known athlete, politician, musician, artist, writer, or other famous person. Or write about someone impor-

tant to you personally such as a relative, teacher, minister, or friend. Whomever you pick, you must sincerely hold in high esteem. Turn the person into a nice giant using the devices listed above. Whether your tone is serious or humorous, you cannot have fun exaggerating if you do not have truthful, specific details to play upon. Be specific about accomplishments and unique attributes compared to others. Inspect the details of the person's early life or when you first knew the person, then inspect their height of achievement or when the person meant the most to you, and finally, if appropriate, their end or fading influence. This historical frame will give your essay structure. Exaggerate every truthful detail except those few important qualities that make your giant a vulnerable human. In this exaggerated context, these qualities usually show off more on a giant than with anyone else.

7
UGLY GIANTS
Undercutting products or mentalities

One method of countering a product, social mentality, or philosophical point of view is to create a person or place that embodies this item to be undercut, then blow up the person or place like giant balloons so that their details become extravagant, grotesque, and overwhelming. Examples of this below are from Jonathan Swift's *Gulliver's Travels* and Germaine Greer's *The Female Eunuch*.

One of the most direct ways to expand this world that will be deflated, is to draw its people and items in a literally large physical scale. For Jonathan Swift this technique worked par-

FULL-BLOODED STRATEGY

ticularly well in Part II, "The Voyage to Brobdingnag," where Gulliver, the normal-sized human being in the book, meets and comments on the giants that live in Brobdingnag. One of the many things that Swift torches in *Gulliver's Travels* is human vanity, including our glorification of our bodies; so by blowing humans up to be giants, he is able to show us ourselves microscopically close, closer than we would ever want to see. Through Gulliver's observations, Swift cures the reader of wonderful-body syndrome by rubbing the reader's face in realities that usually humans can turn away from, or at least consider small enough to be abberrations: "There was a woman with a cancer in her breast, swelled to a monstrous size, full of holes, in two or three of which I could have easily crept, and covered my whole body. There was a fellow with a wen in his neck, larger than five woolpacks ... But, the most hateful sight of all was the lice crawling on their clothes. I could see with my naked eye ... their snouts with which they rooted like swine."

Swift also slaps us for our food obsessions well before we can even consider gluttony as a grotesquerie. In this land of giants "the Queen (who had indeed but a weak stomach) took up at one mouthful as much as a dozen English farmers could eat at a meal," and "She would craunch the wing of a lark, bones and all, between her teeth, although it were nine times as large as that of a fullgrown turkey." If that is not enough to slow down food consumption and undercut our fastidious discrimination about the food we eat and the decorum with which we surround table manners, the giant flies in Brobdingnag will: "They would sometimes alight upon my victuals, and leave their loathsome excrement or spawn behind, which to me was very visible, though not to the natives of that country, whose large optics were not so acute as mine in viewing smaller objects."

Swift can ruin even the most natural indulgences. Nothing stirs the male sexual imagination more, or brings more sexual pride to women who count on them to lure men, than female breasts. It is only human that these fleshy appendages always have been idealized, but lest they occupy too much room in our fantasies, Swift blows them out of proportion, and then pops the image:

"It stood prominent six foot, and could not be less than sixteen in circumference. The nipple was about half the bigness of my head, and the hue both of that and the dug so varified with spots, pimples and freckles, that nothing could appear more nauseous ... This made me reflect upon the fair skins of our English ladies, who appear so beautiful to us, only because they are of our own size ..." And later when Gulliver experiences what beforehand might be considered the ultimate in sensual relaxation, stripped naked and laid the full length of a woman's breast, "he was much disgusted; because, to say the truth, a very offensive smell came from their skins; which I do not mention or intend to the disadvantage of those excellent ladies, for whom I have all manner of respect; but I conceive that my sense was more acute in proportion to my littleness, and that those illustrious persons were no more disagreeable to their lovers, or to each other, than people of the same quality are with us in England."

Greer exaggerates in a different way. She wants to shatter the stereotypic self-indulged woman. One way she does this, is to talk about this kind of woman in terms of a single person (she) rather than as a group of women (they), so that when long lists of examples are given of all the items these women want collectively, for a split second the reader associates all the items weighted down on one person. The one person here is a giant vacuum cleaner of a woman, sucking up all that the natural world has to offer: "She is the crown of creation, the masterpiece. The depths of the sea are ransacked for pearl and coral to deck her; the bowels of the earth are laid open that she might wear gold, sapphires, diamonds, and rubies. Baby seals are battered with staves, unborn lambs ripped from their mothers' wombs, millions of moles, muskrats, squirrels, minks, ermines, foxes, beavers, chincillas, ocelots, lynxes, and other small and lovely creatures die untimely deaths that she might have furs. Egrets, ostriches and peacocks, butterflies and beetles yield her their plumage."

When Greer paints this one woman with all the cosmetic items that women buy and splices all the images of advertisements together to create this mythological woman, she creates one giant, plastic doll: "Her glossy lips and mat complexion, her un-

FULL-BLOODED STRATEGY

focused eyes and flawless fingers, her extraordinary hair all floating shining, curling and gleaming, reveal the inhuman triumph of cosmetics, lighting, focusing and printing, cropping and composition. She sleeps unruffled, her lips red and juicy and closed, her eyes as crisp and black as if new painted, and her false lashes immaculately curled. Even when she washes her face with a new creamier toilet soap her expression is as tranquil and vacant and her paint as flawless as ever."

The most extravagant device Greer uses is to turn "my lady" into a goddess, in that the forces of nature actually conspire for her: "The sun shines only to burnish her skin and gild her hair; the wind blows only to whip up the color in her cheeks; the sea strives to bathe her; flowers die gladly so that her skin may luxuriate in their essence." The world becomes a servant to Greer's giant.

WORK OUT

Using either Swift's or Greer's method or a combination of both, make fun of a product, social mentality, or philosophical point of view. You need a person or place to embody the thing you want to investigate and undercut. Then visualize this person or place in a Swiftian land of giants. For instance, visit giant versions of a miserable fast food franchise, a locker room crowded with full-of-themselves jocks, a convention of existential philosophers or feminists, a place of religious worship, a political caucus room, a computer hack, a cut-rate department store, a kennel that takes care of expensive dogs, or a doctor's office. Imagine that everything is so large that at human scale you can see things the giants cannot see or that they take for granted, since to them these details are almost a visual blur. (Maybe aside from physical details, even their words and sentences are so giant that you can get lost in them and notice things they are saying more carefully than they do.) Try to keep a flat objective tone like Swift does: you cannot help what you see, you are just reporting.

If you concentrate on using Greer's method, consider some of the same subjects listed above, but concentrate on building long lists of items and write in the third person singular (he, she, or it). For instance, embody all prideful athletes in one person and discuss all the things "he" eats, "he" drinks, "he" wears, and words "he" uses in discussing feats, or flirting with the opposite sex, or commanding his cronies. Combine all the details that you notice in numerous, different kinds of prideful athletes, into one person.

Whichever method you use, it is crucial to gather a slew of details about the world you are countering. Do library research if necessary, casual interviews with proponents of the world you are going to pop, and be sure to visit the real world version that you are undercutting. You will notice details you took for granted before now that you know you are going to expand that world.

Whichever method you use to exaggerate, remember that your satire will not ring true unless the details you blow up or compound are themselves based on truth and reality. If they are not, then the exaggeration will simply make your lack of objectivity or carelessness in observation seem more obvious.

8
THIRTEEN WAYS OF LOOKING AT A BLACKBIRD
Capturing complex subjects

"Thirteen Ways of Looking at a Blackbird" is the title of a poem by the well known American poet and insurance executive, Wallace Stevens. In the poem, Stevens looks at blackbirds in thirteen different ways, through thirteen very short, two to seven line stanzas numbered from one to thirteen. Teacher and poet Kenneth Koch has pointed out that some of the stanzas make the blackbird part of a prophecy: "O thin men of Haddam,/ Why do you imagine golden birds?/ Do you not see how the blackbird/ Walks around the feet/ Of the women about you?" In other stanzas the blackbird seems smaller, still magical yet dwarfed by landscapes: "Among twenty snowy mountains/ The only moving thing/ Was the eye of the blackbird." In some stanzas the bird is part of a story: "He rode over Connecticut/ In a glass coach./ Once, a fear pierced him,/ In that he mistook/ The shadow of his equipage/ For blackbirds." In others, like where "A man and a woman and a blackbird/ Are one," the bird seems to be solely a spiritual abstraction.

The excitement generated by looking at a common object almost simultaneously from widely disparate angles in order to round out its complexity, is not new. Art historian E.H. Gombrich argues that ancient Egyptian artists worried much more about completeness than prettiness, and therefore did not paint what could be seen at a given moment from a confined angle of vision, but rather painted all important angles at once. Just as the blackbird in Steven's poem is seen from thirteen dramatic shifts in angles, the Egyptian depiction of man was shown from at least three angles, forming a more accurate, thorough reality, one more complete than normally pictured by the limited organisms trapped in our skulls' sockets. The totality of the human eye and torso are seen most completely from a frontal view; so that is how Egyptian artists portray them, but the rest of the face, and the arms and legs in movement, are more vivid from a profile angle. Furthermore, the foot has more definition viewed from the inside of the sole, a view uncluttered by fragments of smaller toes. So these side and inside views were combined with the frontal view of the eye and torso in one drawing. Any depiction more comfortable to the eye, in other words any line of vision limited to one angle, would be incomplete, jeopardizing accurate identification of the person, and risking their reception of entitled offerings when they died.

One year in *New York* magazine Peter Blaunder compiled seventy-nine, stanza-like viewpoints on the subject of New York style, effectively Egyptianizing the reality of the city in a manner that could not be accomplished in a more unified, easy-on-the-mind's-eye essay. Just as Stevens was able to use varied stanzas to build the complex unseen reality of the simple blackbird, Blaunder uses the dramatic jolts of diverse points of views expressed through disparate styles to capture the full reality of a

FULL-BLOODED STRATEGY

city as complex as New York. For instance, in one sense New York style is intangible, and some of the compiled angles turn it into an abstraction. In his "stanza," Michael Korda says "New York Style is being too busy to think about style," and Eddie Jaffe says "New York Style: You never have to ask what it is. You see it and know it. If you don't know it, it isn't New York Style."

Others point out the exotic, bizarre juxtapositions in New York style. Novelist Jay McInerney finds that "New York continues to turn Japanese ... The package is becoming the product. Appearances are filing for divorce from meanings." Gay Talese says "New York is a city of contrast and tension — wearing a diamond watch in the subway with a Luger in your pocket while reading the *Wall Street Journal*." Morley Safer notices a complex triumvirate of influence: "New York style is quite simply the distillation of every aspect of human existence to just three things: food, sex, and the weather. In any given week, a stylish New Yorker will face a crisis of all three and will tell everyone — his hairdresser, her stockbroker, and their caterer." Painter Larry Rivers chooses to point out a ride on a graffiti-filled subway and notices "It was insanity. People standing there with all this black spaghetti twirling on the walls behind them."

Some of the "stanzas" are very literal and long like William Buckley's which continues for a whole column, and some are literal and very short like Isaac Bashevis Singer's who only can say one word, "RUSH." On the other hand, some respond best completely in metaphor. John Chancelor says "The avenues in my neighborhood are Pride, Covetousness, and Lust; the cross streets are Anger, Gluttony, Envy, and Sloth. I live over on Sloth, and the style on our street is to avoid the other thoroughfares." Many like David Mamet talk in terms of a small story, like the glass coach stanza in the blackbird poem. Mamet's story captures the nervous coarseness of New York style: "I was down in the village recently on a very rainy day when a cab pulled up at a light. A young man and a woman started to get out with their baby as the light turned green, and a second car pulled up behind them. The man in the second car got out and started yelling, 'Are you out of your f mind? Are you out of your f. . . . . . mind?' That is New York style."

Some like Grace Paley point to the foreign influence of New York, "the city of neighborhoods. Bronx, Brooklyn, Queens, my world of childhood repeated in different languages and different colors," or James Morton, Dean of St. John the Divine, who remembers a 40 foot Christmas tree with unusual decorations, "2,000 origami paper cranes folded by New York schoolchildren as part of a tradition started in Hiroshima by an eleven-year-old girl who was dying from radiation and made the first such cranes on her deathbed."

The serious angles of vision are balanced by ironic ones such as Yogi Berra's: "There's no place like New York. If you're talking about baseball, the fans are the best and the most knowledgeable. They cheer the other team if they play well and they boo you if you don't. I've been treated very well here." And finally, some such as Annie Flanders's have angles within their angle: "Tuxedos in the daytime and sunglasses at night. Earning off the books and learning on the job. Being invited to a party you can't get into and getting into a part you weren't invited to. A pair of worn jeans and a $900 belt. A limo to the airport and a budget flight to Rome. Downtown luring uptown and uptown luring downtown. Dressing white in winter and dressing black in summer. Not caring and caring desperately. Makeup on boys and crew cuts on girls. Nine to 5 P.M. and 9 to 5 A.M. New York."

WORK OUT

Many essays explore an argument, issue, or item from different angles but usually through a single voice with smooth transitions that lead the reader from one viewpoint to another. But to a certain extent, it is more honest and more exciting to represent those angles through different methods and styles, jolting the reader to and fro, forcing him or her to experience the subject's complexity, not just read about it.

In a short essay, write at least thirteen short paragraphs about a single subject that you feel is often too complicated to discuss or argue such as an emotion, a city, a person, a philosophical viewpoint, or a book. Each paragraph should cover a distinct point of view or vision on your subject and be written in a completely different style appropriate to that paragraph's content. You can leave extra space between the paragraphs to set off their differences.

Consider writing some paragraphs in a very literal style, others with more metaphor; some very, very short, others longer; some like a miniature story, others like an important statement; some very serious, others humorous or ironic; some very mundane, others very spiritual. Think about how different people might look at the same subject matter differently. (William Faulkner does this in some of his novels such as *The Sound and the Fury* and *As I Lay Dying,* and *Mad Magazine* sometimes uses a blank-as-seen-by-his-blank format to comically juxtapose what different people think of the same person, such as the babysitter as seen by the wife, the babysitter as seen by the twelve year old boy, the babysitter as seen by the two year old.) The finished piece will surround the complexity of your subject and point of view in a way virtually impossible to achieve through a single toned and focused essay.

9
SLICED PIE
Simplifying complex subjects

Many people, including ancient Oriental philosophers and Western alchemists, have symbolized the unity of all matter with the circle because it is self-contained, harmonious, and complete. It does not have opposing or irregular sides, nor a beginning or an end. However, this universal "All," represented by the circle, can be sliced up in different ways. The ancient Chinese grouped the elements of life into two opposing but integrated principles: one called *Yang,* symbolic of activity, reason, and the celestial; the other *Yin,* symbolic of passivity, intuition, and the earthly. These two forces were graphically illustrated by dividing the circle with an "S" curve that created two twisting droplets,

FULL-BLOODED STRATEGY

one forming the inside of the other, and one droplet white to represent *Yang*, the other black to represent *Yin*.

Yang-Yin is one of the most all-encompassing ways to surround and divide the pulse of the universe. Having life split into two primary principles helps us to contemplate more clearly what is otherwise a whirl-wind of complex, universal forces. But there is more than one way to slice life or any part of life. When a writer is able to perceive that specific details within any part of life cluster together to form different groups, then the writer can hold those clusters together, surrounding them with unique labels. This polarizing of reality pulls together details otherwise scattered or blurred out of focus by life's complexities.

For instance, in his book *The Anatomy of Destructiveness*, social scientist Eric Fromm is interested in personality traits. After years of observing human beings, he notices that people break into two basic categories, those that are necrophilous and those that are biophilous.

Necrophilia in its extreme form is characterized by a desire to sexually abuse corpses, and a general love of dead ideas and drained souls. Usually necrophilia is expressed through more subtle traits: a passion to transform something that is alive into something stale, an impulse to solve problems with force, or a marked focus on sickness, failure, and a dark prognosis for the future. Other times it is marked by even more subtle traits. For instance, a necrophilious person may display indifference towards favorable change, enthusiasm, or internal growth in others; become lifeless in conversation despite the person's intelligence and education, or the interest of the subject itself. The person may demonstrate an obsession with the past, material things, regulations, or institutions and, on a more personal level, may be capable only of flashing self-conscious grins rather than spontaneous laughter. In general, a necrophilous person would have a cerebral orientation with flattened feelings, and be capable of having a personal reaction only with a great deal of difficulty.

Biophilia has the opposite characteristics: a preference for construction, the new, and adventure at the expense of retention, confirmation, the old, and certainty; an ability to see the whole and not just parts; a belief in molding through love, reason, and example rather than through force or rules; and a vision of the Good as being a reverence for life.

Both of Fromm's categories fuse together important character traits that otherwise would be blended into a dense social landscape. By connecting details through the focus of a special category, Fromm awakens our insights: if we perceive one necrophilous characteristic, we are on the alert for others.

Categories are focusing tools and never should be thought of as the only way to slice through reality. Depending on one's purpose, one kind of division might be more helpful than another. A biologist needs to know that mammals divide into three groups: those almost extinct ones that lay eggs (Protheria), those that are pouched (Metatheria), and those that are placental (Eutheria). But an artist might consider some of Jorge Luis Borges's categories of animals from "The Analytical Language of John Wilkins" more valuable. Some of Borges's animal divisions, such as "those that are included in this classification" or "others," take pie slicing to an extreme, perhaps as a reminder that much of life is not so easily surrounded. But some have interesting visual implications, including "those that belong to the Emperor," "embalmed ones," "fabulous ones," "those that tremble as if they were mad," "those drawn with a very fine camel's hair brush," and "those that resemble flies from a distance." Borges's categories give importance to animal clusters otherwise overlooked. An artist familiar with them might wonder how to draw an animal so that it does not look embalmed or might consider which animals are best drawn with a fine camel's hair brush and which are not.

More than anything, Borges's categories are a reminder that life and learning are always made fresh again, and new insights are made possible when a complex maze of material is regrouped into new divisions. For instance, the study of literature has

FULL-BLOODED STRATEGY

usually been in terms of historical or geographical groupings, focusing on how the literature of a given country changes against different historical backdrops. But new insights are gained by dividing the very same world of literature into other categories: literature with a comic spirit, literature that is dream-like, literature with strong Biblical allusions, literature in which both adults and children find something of value, and literature that is mythic. With these categories, time and geography are transcended to bring together pieces of literature that otherwise could not come together. Bringing them together clarifies different values and purposes of literature that before were not easily perceived.

Sometimes, once an aspect of life is broken into general categories, it is helpful to slice those groups into subgroups. For instance in her book *Break-up: The Core of Modern Art,* Katharine Kuh slices the art of our century off from others because it is "characterized by shattered surfaces, broken color, segmented compositions, dissolving forms and shredded images. Curiously insistent is this consistent emphasis on break-up." But within this general classification of art, Kuh knows that there are subgroups, each sharing the characteristics of the general group, but also possessing or emphasizing more specialized concerns that differentiate the subgroups from each other. Two examples include the subgroup Cubism, characterized by "arbitrarily rearranging transparent planes and surfaces so that all sides of an object could be seen at once," and Surrealism, characterized by "splintered time sequence with an abandon borrowed from the world of fragmented dreams" with content "unhinged," "allowing disconnected episodes to recreate the disturbing life of our unconscious."

One of the most interesing sliced pies with its pieces sliced again into subgroups, was done by Arnold Mandell, a psychiatrist. In an article entitled "A Psychiatric Study of Professional Football," Mandell summarized his insights having studied the San Diego Charger football team for over a year. First Mandell noticed that that the pie could be sliced in half. The cut was between the personalities of the offensive players, who perform prearranged, carefully choreographed plays to move the ball, and defensive players, whose function is to interrupt the other team's attempt to move the ball. He found that offensive players had clean and orderly lockers, liked structure, discipline, and repetition, and tended to be conservative. Defensive players had messy lockers ("the better the defensive player, the bigger the mess"), could not stand structure, and challenged "rules or regulations put forward by anybody, anyplace."

Within each of these two general categories, Mandell broke the players into subgroups by position. For instance, there were four subgroups for offensive players including linemen ("ambitious, tenacious, precise ... toughness that I would call stubborn rather than explosive ... sacrificial"), wide receivers ("narcissistic and vain, and basically loners ... disciplined"), running backs, and quarterbacks. Then all of these groups were sliced again into even more specific groups, sometimes according to a more specific position, other times simply by the fact that there are two types of players for the same position.

For instance, all quarterbacks have a "self-confidence that is more akin to super-arrogance" and have "sheer courage." But quarterbacks break down into two more specific groups: "One is that of the naturally arrogant man who does not feel bound by the rules governing other men. He makes his own. He exploits the environment in a tough, tricky way and with very little compunction;" the other rules "with assurance from On High, sometimes with humility but always with a religious commitment that helps "insulate him from what was obviously a particularly stressful situation." Mandell wondered if either quarterback does well though when plays are called from the bench and predicted a third kind of quarterback for this situation.

After breaking down the offense into groups and subgroups, Mandell went on to break the defensive team into groups and subgroups. In summary, Mandell realized that much of the game is in the mind and therefore suitable personalities for the functions of different roles is of upmost importance; that "players working in the wrong position are uneasy and attempt to cor-

FULL-BLOODED STRATEGY

rect for their uneasiness." At the end of the article Mandell extended the positions, finally turning them into metaphorical labels, by comparing celebrities and personal relations to different positions. Woody Allen became a defensive back, Mandell's mother an offensive lineman, his father a wide receiver, the pianist Leonard Bernstein a cross between a quarterback and wide receiver.

WORK OUT

Pick a large group of people whom you know intimately or whom you can observe first hand: students in your classes, people you have gone out with on dates, people you work with, people you eat with in restaurants or cafeterias, English teachers, people you see on a specific type of vacation, people in a religious congregation or political organization, or children at a park.

Or pick a subject that you know intimately or would like to research: typical novels read in English classes, materials read on vacation, a specific kind of music, a sport, horror films, serious art films, dresses sold at classy stores, clothes worn by arrogant men or sleazy women, places of worship, or kitsch.

Whatever group of people or subject you study, slice it into two major parts, writing about each section in two separate long paragraphs that explain and describe the major characteristics of each slice. Give each of the two divisions an intriguing label that the reader will enjoy remembering and using and that will reflect the essence of each group. Have fun inventing the labels; they should not sound like anything you have ever heard before. See Chapter 4 of Part I on metaphor for ideas but avoid the problems of labeling mentioned in Chapter 5 of Part I on making faces. However, playful use of metal mask can be amusing. For instance, there is a *New Yorker* magazine cartoon where a wife who is hosting a large dinner party turns to her husband and says "Oh dear! I put all the postarticulates on the same side of the table."

Then take one of your two large slices and divide it again into three subgroups, each one having the characteristics you have written about above. But without repeating those characteristics, spend a short paragraph on each one of the three subgroups describing and explaining the details that make each subgroup distinct from one another. Invent three original labels for each of these groups.

10
STRIP TEASE
Narrowing towards truth and revelation

One of the most powerful ways to organize material is to mentally wrap a climactic statement, conclusion, or revelation of truth, in all the details that had lead up to such an end, then to pull each detail off very slowly, writing about each one, until gradually the final truth is reached and revealed to the reader. Aside from creating an element of suspense, slowly stripping off details allows the reader to savour them, appreciating them as being just as important as the climax. We usually associate this kind of suspense and savouring of detail with fictional writing, and the first example below provides one of the most effective uses of strip tease in fiction ever written. It is especially effective because the content is literally about sex. But the same strip tease organization is at work in many essays, magazine articles, and business letters. For instance, the second example below, the successful emergence of a particular piece of merchandise from Marvin Kaye's book *A Toy Is Born,* could not be about a more mundane subject.

All fictions, to some extent, are strip teases, since all fictions are the unfolding of details that pull the reader forward to amazing truths about life. Several years ago Raymond Carver wrote a short story entitled "Will You Please Be Quiet, Please?" The story focuses on the husband, Ralph, a high school teacher, and his wife Marian, a community college professor. In eight years of marriage they have two children, and only one serious, looked-at-rationally-seemed-impossible disturbance, which had occurred two years prior to the present time in the story: Ralph "had taken it into his head one night at a party that Marian had betrayed him with Mitchell Anderson, a friend."

Like most good fiction, the story builds to revealing, unexpected climaxes of truth. One is that his wife did betray him that night two years ago. The other more important one is that, after Ralph finds this out, then wanders around in a night filled with physical and psychological confusion and comes home to his wife without knowing how to respond to her, Ralph finally makes a "momentous discovery" about himself. In the split seconds after turning to respond to Marian's affectionate caresses in bed, Ralph finds himself in Marian's eyes: "Then, as he gazed even deeper, he glimpsed in first one pupil and then the other, the cameo-like, perfect reflection of his own strange and familiar face."

This revelation is the most important one in the story, but the section of Carver's story where the sexual betrayal is first revealed, provides the clearest, most graphic example of strip tease. The whole scene develops very slowly, starting with a visit by the Franklins (who had been at a party where Marian had gotten drunk and left with the slender, slightly pocked-faced Mitchell Anderson). This visit reminds Marian of the party and so,

FULL-BLOODED STRATEGY 113

absorbed in the midst of domestic chores, she innocently asks Ralph if he remembers the party. The strip tease for the reader, and for Ralph himself, has begun.

A period of silence follows; then Ralph asks for the first time in two years if Anderson kissed her. Marian responds with an I-didn't-say-that but Ralph apologizes for her with a it-was-a-long-time-ago, prodding her on until she admits yes, "a few times." At this point Carver, has the reader believing that the unwrapping of truth might be over. Ralph sounds cool, acting like an unwrap never started. Inside he desperately wants to believe that at worst the unwrap is over, that all the truth is now revealed.

But Carver has just begun. There are more details to strip away. Ralph becomes defensive: "You said he only put his arm around you while he was driving." Then, in a flash-back Carver reveals that that night Ralph had hit Marian in the mouth, she had responded by saying she had not done anything. Now, remembering that night, they both apologize for doing wrong, wondering how they ever got on this subject, and again the unwrapping of truth appears to be over. A calm ensues with Marian volunteering to make some buttered rums. But the reader has been teased again. Ralph asks what else went on because "it's all right to talk about it now."

She insists nothing went on, but Ralph keeps insisting that it is okay to talk about it because of the time lapse. He maintains a "reasoning quality" to his voice until she says she doesn't want to talk about it. Ralph insists angrily that she admit all, to which she responds with a sub-unwrap: a story about her being drunk, the host's kitchen being out of booze, Anderson's being "very witty about it all," leaving on an impulse to the liquor store. As the realization of betrayal becomes more intense, Ralph's anger mounts. Marian refuses to go on, but Ralph keeps insisting he will not be angry; in fact promises he won't, and so Marian continues with the details leading up to Anderson's kissing her breast. Ralph is both erotically aroused by the stripping of details and angry enough to smash Marian in the face.

By the time the scene is over, so much stripping away at truth has occurred, that Ralph is no longer in a panic to find out if Marian and Anderson had had sexual intercourse, (by now he knows they had), but in utter anguish, desperately looking for any kind of consolation, asks if she let him "come" in her. A writer cannot strip down details any further than that. No writer can build them up as thick and then strip them off any more carefully than that.

A written piece about merchandise might not seem to have the same dramatic possibilities as sexual betrayal, but in his piece on Silly Putty, Marvin Kaye effectively strip teases the reader nonetheless. He does not interest the reader in this "toy with one moving part" by describing the magic of what silly putty can do, since he knows most readers are familiar with its ability to stretch, shatter, pick up newsprint, mold, flow, and bounce, although he quickly reminds us of these attributes at the beginning of the piece. Instead he dramatizes the sequence of accidents that shaped Silly Putty as a marketable product. One detailed incident is pulled off of another until finally Silly Putty is revealed as a fullfledged merchandise success story.

The first accident is that in 1945 General Electric was experimenting with synthetic rubber for the war effort when an engineer happened to drop boric acid into a test tube with silicone oil. The "accident" bounced. In a single line paragraph, Kaye savours and dramatizes the incident. He declares, *"Accident number one: Silly Putty is born."* There are many more details to strip away though before Silly Putty is a reality. In the next section of the chapter, Kaye outlines the history of Peter Hodgson, a man who leaves home to explore the marketing profession, has the opportunity to sell everything from a presidential candidate to tires, fails as a research consultant, other jobs and his marriage collapse, and at the nadir of his career he becomes part of *"Accident number two:"* he is hired by a New Haven toy shop to publish its catalogue. He decides to include a page of toys for grown ups, while at the same time GE's mystery goo is becoming a conversation piece at cocktail parties. The reader wonders what accident will bring goo and man together. Eventually Ruth Fall-

FULL-BLOODED STRATEGY 115

gatter, who introduced Hodgson to the toy business, now introduces him to Silly Putty. All these details are explored carefully by Kaye. This holds the reader back to savour each one, and strains the reader, forcing him or her to wonder now how and when the final marraige of Silly Putty with the public will finally come.

The details continue to unfold: Hodgson notices adult business men play with the goo even as they talk about it being useless as a product; so he takes a chance and sells it. The chemical toy outsells virtually everything in the catalogue. The story of success seems over, but this layer of success is only a mild tease. Hodgson tries to get his employer to manufacture it but she refuses. He puts it on the market himself but runs into packaging problems. *"Accident number three:"* Economic necessity forces Hodgson to encase his product in plastic 'eggs'..." The packaging is a success; orders mount. Doubleday orders a few dozen, a few weeks later a gross, this changes to two gross, four gross, and finally five hundred a day. A writer for *New Yorker* drops in to buy one for a friend and ends up doing an article on it. Sales bounce all over the place.

The success story finally appears to be unwrapped but then the writer throws in a negative accident: the Korean war. There is a clamp down on defense materials used in Silly Putty practically forcing Hodgson out of business. It takes him two years traveling to every state in the Union to rebuild demand. But now another thread unravels. Kids start buying Silly Putty and the market swings in an unexpected direction. It takes ten years to solve the problem of quality control for kids. The product now has to detach from human hair and carpets. Not until the 1960's does the product finally emerge again resulting in $6.3 million a year in sales. Only at this point is the package totally unwrapped for the reader.

WORK OUT
Think of an incident in your life that evolved slowly, finally resulting in an unpredictable end or revelation. The incident might have involved your love life, a problem in your family, an

athletic event you watched, a work of art, drama, or paper you worked on, a conflict where you work, or a legal problem. Before organizing your piece, write down everything that leads up to the conclusion. You need lots of wrapping material. Consider both details that you knew at the time might be important to the final outcome, and details that you know are important only in retrospect. Maybe even write down details that are not literally important to the final outcome, but foreshadow it in symbolic ways: messages on billboards and posters, a line in an irrelevant letter sitting on a table, dialogue in another room or on televison, or a song lyric on the radio.

Now start the paper. Unwrap each detail carefully, forcing the reader to savour them. Tease the reader, giving special emphasis to those details that seem to conclude the incident. One way to do this is to include those quiet details or moments that build tension before the next important development just as Carver does in the short story. Another way is to actually call attention to developments the way Kaye does by labeling certain incidents as accidents.

By the time you reach your final revelation or conclusion, the reader will be totally absorbed in it, and more important, will find the conclusion credible, no matter how surprising it is, because the reader will have experienced the way the final revelation or outcome gradually came into being.

11
FLASHBACK
Intensifying reflection

Usually when we discuss something that happened in the past, we use the past tense: people in the past walked, talked, ate, loved, and fought. But sometimes life's pulse becomes much stronger when past events are narrated as if they are happening in the present time. When a writer looks at the past in terms of the present, we join that writer in a very special reality where events seem both unreal, haunted by a backwards movement through time possible only in dreams; and also super real, outlined with a clarity obtained only when considering events in retrospect.

Two key examples of this dream walk into the past are by the writer, editor, and teacher, Delmore Schwartz, in his story "In Dreams Begin Responsibilities," and former Ambassador to the Soviet Union, George Kennan's look at history in his *New Yorker* article, "Flashbacks."

In his story, Schwartz, or his fictional persona, watches his parents in their youthful past, awkwardly trying to wrap up their courtship with a marriage proposal. Knowing one's parents in the past, before they become parents, is always a surprise, if not a shock. Everyone's perception of parents is colored by the time span that begins with one's own birth. A child seeing parents earlier, still struggling to know themselves and each other, as well as untouched by their unborn children, would be unsettled. They would no longer be parents; they would be strangers. Schwartz intensifies this "parental" past, bringing it into the present, by putting it on a movie screen and putting himself in the audience: "I think it is the year 1909. I feel as if I were in a moving-picture theater, the long arm of light crossing the darkness and spinning, my eyes fixed upon the screen."

The father arrives at the house of the mother's family. Since this is happening on a movie screen, Schwartz can watch the arrival, the greetings, and all the following interactions, with the objectivity of someone outside a dream looking in. But what makes the situations especially haunting and sometimes horrifying, is that emotions, actions, or words that usually would by now be dismissed, or at least softened, into embarrassing blunders of time past, are made fresh again through the potency of the present tense. The present tense also makes the past more urgent: it still seems warm enough to be reshaped. We and the persona feel we can still do something. The past does not seem decided yet.

Therefore we and the persona are especially discouraged to learn on the movie screen that the mother and father "are not yet engaged and he [the father] is not yet sure that he loves my mother, so that, once in a while, he becomes panicky about the bond already established." The reader would not have been so troubled if this past had been written with verbs connoting the past: "They were not yet engaged and he was not yet sure that he loved my mother, so that, once in a while, he became panicky about the bond already established." Making the action definitely in the past keeps the reader at ease because the reader can subconsciously rationalize that either time must have partially resolved such unpleasant dilemmas or if not, there is nothing anyone can do now.

All the other painful details of the courtship would also have been time-washed and dissolved if written about in the past tense, but instead they stay in the solid state of the anxious present, including such embarrassing details as the father pumping up his own ego as he "thinks about himself in the future and so arrives at the place he is to visit in a mild state of exaltation;" the fact that "the respect in which my father is held in this house is tempered by a good deal of mirth;" the concern of the grandfather who "is worried; he is afraid that my father will not make a good husband for his oldest daughter;" the prideful mother who, with her hand on the father's arm as she tells him about a novel that he belittles as "sugary," "feels satisfied by the interest she has awakened; and is showing my father how intelligent she is and how interesting." It is hard enough knowing these things happened in the past; it is unbearable to see them happening "right now."

Several times Schwartz or his persona interrupts the film with weeping and even shouting, begging his parents not to get married. By the end of their day, the mother's stubborness and father's impatience ends with the two quarreling and separating. Furthermore, Schwartz's alter-ego is now near hysteria, shouting "What are they doing?," while the movie theatre's usher drags him out, warning him to be more tolerant: "You cannot carry on like this, it is not right, you will find that out soon enough, everything you do matters too much." The tension of this past in this filmed present is finally interrupted by the story teller's awakening, finding he had been riveted to celluloid dreams within a dream, and that now the morning of his own twenty-first birthday had "already begun."

George Kennan is both a close-up eyewitness observer and historian of a changing period of Soviet-American relations from the early thirties until he is forced out of the American Ambassadorship in 1952. Before he drops back in time, he actually explains the advantages of flash backs or writing about the past in terms of the present: "To stress the responsibility of these memories in speaking for themselves and to distance the young man who received the experiences from the elderly one who now recalls them, I take the liberty of putting them in the narrative present." Kennan starts each large section of his article with a sentence that clearly states he is flashing back to a specific point of time, always keeping the particular scene in the present: "Let us jump ahead now to the days, fifty-one years ago this past November ...," "Another change of scene," "Let us jump ahead again," "The scene shifts to Washington ...," "Next picture."

Kennan starts in 1932 with a description of Russia in present tense that "is right out of Tolstoy," an "older Russia which I shall never see again in the flesh." This quick glance to the future, admitting that the old Russia he is experiencing now will soon disappear, while he describes fleeting, present moments, makes the present reality especially intense. When Kennan cuts into the present with the future, we are reminded that the present is simply a grain of sand in the flow of time. The moments become more special.

One of Kennan's most powerful flashbacks involves the horrors of the Stalinist purges. They begin in 1937 and the first American Ambassador to communist Russia is replaced by a new Ambassador, "a shallow and politically ambitious man, who knows nothing about Russia." Kennan has been acting as interpreter and diplomatic secretary. Despite Kennan's explanations while the two sit at a great public purge trial, the Ambassador "understands nothing of what is really going on. He even thinks the accused are genuinely guilty of the preposterous charges to which they are confessing, and he sententiously pronounces this opinion, during the intermission, to the assembled American journalists."

FULL-BLOODED STRATEGY

But Kennan understands the hidden agenda. Again he describes it in the present: "But I do know what is going on; and the sight of these ashen, doomed men, several of them only recently prominent figures of the regime but now less than twenty-four hours away from their executions — the sight of these men standing there mumbling their preposterous confessions in the vain hope of saving themselves, or perhaps the members of their families, from disaster, the sight of their twitching lips, their prison pallor, their evasive downcast eyes — is never to leave my memory." This last reference to the future in terms of the present's lasting power in the memory, helps to underline the potency of that present.

Kennan describes many other dramatic historical moments experienced in his official positions. One of the best reasons Kennan has for writing about all these events in the present instead of the past is that he feels final outcomes are not as important as what people know in their lives to be true at the present time. He knows that principal historical characters "are all actors in what will ultimately be seen as a tragic drama; but I try to judge them for what they were, and for what they knew."

WORK OUT

Write an essay narrating a past event of either personal or historical importance. Personal subjects could be about a past love affair, a telling incident with your parents, an unusual experience you had traveling, or a time when you discovered the truth about an institution that you had always thought differently about. Historical events could include subjects you have recently studied in history classes or ones you would like to research, combining documents, biographies, and history texts.

Most important, make sure that you consider your material to be special because you are going to write about it in the present tense, as if the event were occurring right now. This will make the material intense and this in turn will have the reader anticipating important, insightful, or suspenseful content. If you do not deliver on one of these, your flashback or flashbacks will get blurry and maybe dissolve.

If you need to, you may skip over large periods of time, flashing back only on key moments, but make it very clear to the reader that you are doing so, using sentences that mark each new flashback: "The scene shifts to last November," "New picture," or "Moving a year ahead." Like Kennan, you may analyze details of the event, but only in terms of quick glances to the future where you mention that the moment you are describing will have an unexpected outcome or unforeseen impact. This will give your essay prophetic intensity. You may also choose, like Schwartz, to view this past event in a dream, always keeping the narration in present time just as it would be in a real dream about the past.

12
DOUBLE EXPOSURES
Revealing double-layered realities

There is a scene in Woody Allen's film *Annie Hall* where Alvie Singer is getting acquainted with Annie. They converse with one another, using a discussion about photography as an excuse to stumble through their artistic credentials. After Annie mentions that she "dabbles" in photography, Alvie shows off his intellectual prowess by verifying that her photos have "a quality." Annie meets the compliment, saying "well I'd like to take a serious photography course." Alvie keeps the discussion high level: "Photography is interesting because it's a new art form and a set of aesthetic criteria have not emerged yet." Annie unintentionally deflates Alvie's pretension: "Set of criteria? You mean if it's a good photo or not?" Alvie one-ups her: "The medium enters in as a condition of the art form itself." Annie counters with her own criteria, remarking that for her its "all instinctive." Alvie is too far into pedantic quicksand to back off: "Still you need a set of guidelines to put it in a social perspective."

But juxtaposed over this lofty, stumbling conversation is another discussion. Both characters talk to themselves in silent thoughts revealed only to the audience in subtitles. These interior mumbles candidly express insecurities and desires too startling for new acquaintances to reveal to each other. For instance, Annie calls herself a yo-yo for using the word "dabble," worries that she is not smart enough for Alvie, and then worries that he may turn out to "be a schmuck like all the others." Meanwhile, the subtitles show Alvie thinking what a good looking girl Annie is, wondering what she must look like naked, and also considering that he doesn't know what he is talking about, worrying that she senses he is shallow, and that he has turned himself into an FM radio talk show.

The audience enjoys the shock of watching the real, interior, subtitled reality humorously juxtaposed with the official, oral, acted reality. Woody Allen, the writer-director, has created a verbal double exposure of two realities. While we experience the first reality, the second immediately undercuts it.

Written double exposure is the consistent splicing together of two different realities, both realities concerned with the same issue. Double exposures provide an effective way to contrast two viewpoints: one usually theoretical, general or official; the other more realistic, specific, or candid. Double exposures are telling because, while reading a piece that makes use of them, the reader is constantly reminded of how numbing, vague, or seductive one version of reality is in comparison to the other.

A good example of double exposing is found in an article entitled "The Day the Bomb Went Off" by Erwin Knoll and Theodore Postol. About half of the article is written as an objective, matter-of-fact, detailed description of a sunny summer morning in the Chicago area at 11:27 after a twenty-megaton nuclear bomb explodes. Another voice, distinguished by italics and usually lasting for a few paragraphs itself, interrupts the main text after every few paragraphs. This second voice is as cold and objective as the first, but it reports only general scientific facts about nuclear bombs and their after-effects. This second, italicized voice makes no attempt to relate material to a particular, flesh-and-blood situation.

In contrast, the primary voice in the article describes the varying extent of destruction in terms of familiar neighborhoods in the Chicago area. Neighborhoods five miles from Ground Zero include "affluent Evanston to the north, well past working-class Cicero on the west ..." These people are almost as "lucky" as those at Ground Zero who have been immediately evaporated, since here people "experienced instant and painless death from the extreme heat long before the noise and shock wave reached them." Sixteen miles away "in the pleasant western suburb of Hinsdale" people are not so lucky. Paint evaporates off house interiors as children scream, blinded by the flash of the fireball; "an instant later, their skin was charred." Twenty-one miles away, which ironically includes the Argonne National Laboratory instrumental in developing the atomic bomb, researchers gazing into the distance watch the sky fill with the brightness of eighty suns, which instantly blazes their eyes out while their exposed skin blisters into third-degree burns.

Thinking in terms of familiar and particular areas makes the reality of destruction especially graphic and terrifying. The reader is constantly reminded of how much safer flat descriptions are by the interruption of the italicized, scientifically official voice. It is a voice much more caught up in the hypnotic use of numbers: *"The yield of a twenty-megaton bomb is some 1,500 times greater than the yield of the bomb that was dropped on Hiroshima thirty-three years ago."* It is a voice dazed by scientific explanations: *"The enormously high temperatures from the fireball of a nuclear weapon generate enough light and heat to ignite simultaneous fires over huge areas. In these areas the heated air forms a rising column, resembling on a vast scale the air-flow in a fireplace."* Primarily, it is a voice that gives numbing scientific details precedence over human realities: absorbed neutrons lead to production of *"radioactive isotopes of such elements as sodium, chlorine, manganese, zinc, copper..."* With the double exposure of both voices, the reader cannot escape from the realization that it is the second, general-explanation voice that, regardless of how much it discusses destruction, nevertheless helps to disguise the real horrors of nuclear war.

An even more unexpected example of double exposure involves an article on Barbie Dolls published in *The Village Voice* by Gwenda Blair entitled "Boobs in Toyland." In this essay, it is the primary text's voice that is "safe:" It provides a fairly flat explanation for Barbie's social success and a description of "her" economic history. For instance, we learn that for over twenty-five years the 11 1/2" plastic doll has sold well, "one for every female in the United States and Canada." In 1981 retail sales hit $7 billion dollars. We learn that Ruth Handler invented Barbie after watching her own daughter, named Barbie, play with adult fashion dolls and so got the idea of developing a doll with "'fully mature figure' (i.e. breasts, an adult-proportioned head, and permanently arched feet)."

Part of Blair's primary text focuses on the social implications of a Barbie Doll. For instance, she explains that with Barbie, a little girl could "stop changing diapers and start playing out fantasies of her more immediate future as a teenager ... now she had a perfect little woman's body on which to practice all the female arts ..." But after every few paragraphs, scattered throughout the entire essay, Blair creates a double exposure: she abruptly cuts in with italicized quotes from women in their mid to late twenties who had Barbie Dolls. These small italicized quotes are set off in their own paragraphs, and never blended into the primary text with transitions. These second voices contrast with the primary text by being more conversational, and more importantly, by being more willing to be specific and frank about Barbie's part in one's secret life.

For instance, at the end of the discussion on role modeling, we are given the following quote from Delores, 29, artist: *I never*

FULL-BLOODED STRATEGY 127

really liked Barbie. I thought she was snippy and bitchy and when she sat down all she could do was stick her legs straight out. Still, she was so much better than my mother. She was the way I was going to be. A few paragraphs later, Delores cuts in again: *As soon as I got Barbie, I made my old dolls her maids. They just weren't cool enough to play with any more.* Later, just before the primary text mentions that "Barbie also served as a focus for her owner's insecurities, frustrations, and fears," a quote from Paula, 23, a secretary, cuts in: *I resented that Barbie always looked just right, no matter what I did to her, and I was always a mess. And it was so irritating to look at those blank bumps that were her breasts. There was nothing to identify with. First I drew in nipples. Then I bashed them on my nightside table.* And when the primary text coolly points out that Barbie and her male counterpart, Ken, also "provided a certain outlet for her owner's sexual curiosity," other quotes get to the bottom line: *I wasn't sure who was on top and who was on bottom, so instead Ken and Barbie had sex flying through the air. Once I used Ken to masturbate, but then I felt guilty. I was afraid he'd remember* or a comment that *She didn't have homework, she had fun. She knew how to put on a baby voice and giggle and get boys to ask her out. In a way I thought she was a slut, like the girls who danced dirty at school...*

Blair effectively uses double exposure to make us aware of two realities, one having to do with general economic overview and sociological conjecture, the other having to do with secret, private fantasies. Both combine to form a complete picture of the Barbie Doll phenomenon.

WORK OUT

Write about a subject for which you know two versions exist. It is not important that the versions are strongly opposed to one another, but instead that they represent two different attitudes or voices. As with the examples above, one version should be more official or general, the other more realistic and specific. After every few paragraphs of the primary text, abruptly cut in and out with part of the second version. Do not use any transitions, but be sure there is a connection in the content of both versions where they intersect. Put one of the versions in italics. (Words intended for italics get underlined when typing.)

Some possible subjects might include two versions of what a friend did at school, what people did at a social gathering, what happens in a classroom, an English teacher discussing a boring paper with a boring student, a student listening to a boring lecture, who a parent is, what happened in a current news story, a real estate agent selling a house, what a specific vacation is, the importance of a scientific discovery, or your physical appearance.

If you find it difficult to switch back and forth between two kinds of voices, attitudes, and types of support material, first write all of one version and then the other. When you are done, splice one version into the other. The final effect of the double exposure may be to create humor, or to show the weakness of one version compared to the other, or to round out a safe point of view with one that is more threatening.

13
DEVIL'S ADVICE
Spoiling self-righteous arguments

Demands fertilized by others' self-importance or self-righteousness are impositions usually best ignored. Other times, the injustice of these impositions are so suffocating that we are compelled to counter them with straight-forward, well articulated arguments and logic. But often our most reasonable arguments are not taken seriously or ignored: the selfrighteous person or group protects itself, rationalizing that we are socially, politically, culturally, intellectually, or emotionally inferior and unimportant. If we still find such puff-ups to be too insufferable to ignore, there is something else that will get their attention. Give them devil's advice.

Devil's advice involves irony, speaking in words of advice or praise in a way that actually implies blame and disapproval. Writing devil's advice allows a writer to practice a restrained, sardonic sense of humor instead of raging anger. This kind of satire is effective because the advice or praise ignores the protective shield self-importance gives to illogical and questionable motives. It cracks the shield by humorously exaggerating those motives and illogic into a formal proposal, thereby bringing them into an intense light for others. Self-righteous people are usually too tight to appreciate any kind of humor, especially sardonic humor about their own arguments, so the mock praise and advice angers or confuses them. But it does get their attention. Devil's advice does not always pop swollen prides; however, it is usually embarrassing enough to take pride's swell down a bit, and also helps to raise the spirits of others victimized by the person's self-importance.

One of the best examples of devil's advice is entitled "Advice to Youth" delivered by Mark Twain (1835-1910) to students. In it, Twain mentions that he has been asked to talk about something instructive; something, he adds, that will be suitable to "one's tender early years" when advice "will best take root and be most enduring." The very fact that Twain shifts to devil's advice after this solemn opening, might be a mild slap at the pretensions of his academic hosts who ask him to be didactic. The advice itself exposes the youths' real concerns and secret strategies and at the same time makes fun of the worth of parents' advice: "Always obey your parents, when they are present. This is the best policy in the long run, because if you don't they will make you. Most parents think they know better than you do, and you can generally make more by humoring that superstition than you can by acting on your own better judgment."

Twain's attack continues. He wants to embarrass his audience for immoral tendencies he suspects either are going to bud or have already opened in their souls. One of his most obvious leg-pulls concerns lying: "Many a young person has injured himself permanently through a single clumsy and ill-finished lie, the

FULL-BLOODED STRATEGY

result of carelessness born of incomplete training ... the young ought to be temperate in the use of this great art until practice and experience shall give them that confidence, elegance, and precision which alone can make the accomplishment graceful and profitable." Twain goes so far as to take the revered maxim "truth is mighty and will prevail" and demonstrate to the students that the opposite is true, "that a truth is not hard to kill and that a lie told well is immortal." He tells his audience to begin lying early because "If I had begun earlier, I could have learned how by now."

Twain obviously embarrasses anyone who has a tendency to lie because he praises the person's hidden, rationalized excuses for lying. In the rest of the address, Twain covers other aspects of immorality. In his closing remark, he spoils anyone's secret, cynical desire to conform to a corrupt world: "Build your character thoughtfully and painstakingly upon the precepts, and by and by, when you have got it built, you'll be surprised and gratified to see how nicely and sharply it resembles everybody else's."

One of the most icy pieces of devil's advice ever written was in 1729 by Jonathan Swift entitled "A Modest Proposal," a pamphlet that pretends to be a logical proposal for a "fair, cheap, and easy method" to deal with the "prodigious number of children" in Ireland. In actuality, Swift intends to create sympathy for the oppressed, hungry, Irish Catholic peasants, and focus anger on wealthy, bigoted, English absentee landlords and the English aristocracy whose government silently lets the Irish bleed.

In the "modest," logical tone of a benevolent social planner, Swift, or his persona, proposes a plan whereby Irish children instead of "wanting food and raiment for the rest of their lives ... shall on the contrary contribute to the feeding, and partly to the clothing, of many thousands." The plan would also prevent voluntary abortions and the murdering of bastard children, a sacrifice "which would move tears and pity in the most savage and inhuman breast." After a careful analysis of how much it costs to raise a child to the first year, and careful, realistic calculations on how many Irish women are "breeders," Swift gets to the bottom line which he hopes "will not be liable to the least objection": "I have been assured by a very knowing American of my acquaintance in London, that a young healthy child well nursed is at a year old a most delicious, nourishing, and wholesome food, whether stewed, roasted, baked, or boiled; and I make no doubt that it will equally serve in a fricassee or a ragout."

The proposal continues with useful tidbits: "a child will make two dishes at an entertainment for friends;" "the fore or hind quarter will make a reasonable dish ... boiled on the fourth day;" infant's flesh will be in season all year long, but especially in March because "there are more children born in Roman Catholic countries about nine months after Lent;" the carcass may be skinned to make "admirable gloves for ladies, and summer boots for fine gentlemen;" and finally, although it would help to replace abused deer harvests, allowing adolescents into the meat supply would be a mistake since boys would be a tough chew and girls would not be far from becoming breeders themselves, thus "scrupulous people might be apt to censure such a practice (although indeed very unjustly) as a little bordering upon cruelty."

With the same steadiness, Swift's persona outlines the advantages of the proposal, including that "men would become as fond of their wives during the time of their pregnancy as they are now of their mares in foal, their cows in calf, or sows when they are ready to farrow..." Near the end of the essay he dares anyone to advance a proposal that so cheaply solves the hunger problem in Ireland, and requires that anyone who thinks they have one, to first ask the miserable Irish if they do not agree whether they would have been better off sold as food at a year old. In conclusion, Swift's persona professes his sincerity in wanting to relieve the poor and give some pleasure to the rich, since he has no personal interest in the plan, not having "children by which I can propose to get a single penny..."

Swift's essay is successful because, like Twain, he touches what he knows are hidden and not-so-hidden hatreds for the Irish, for-

FULL-BLOODED STRATEGY

malizing those hatreds and arrogance into a proposal so grim that it would be an understatement to say the proposal was an embarrassment to certain English.

Almost fifty years after Swift wrote his "modest" piece, William Blake wrote one of the most passionate pieces of devil's advice ever written, entitled "The Marriage Between Heaven and Hell." Blake's sense of irony is different from Twain's and Swift's. He does not write with tongue-in-cheek, rather with prophetic directness. He is ironic though in that he has Hell represent good, associating it with energy, freedom, delight, and candor, while he has Heaven represent evil, associating it with an assortment of chained restraints ranging from modesty to repression. Actually, Blake believes Heaven and Hell are both necessary, and that without "contraries is no progression." But by advising us to consider the virtues of Hell, he spoils the security of those self-righteous enough to have bought tickets only to Heaven.

Blake's piece is an unusual combination of prose, poetry, and proverbs. One of the most famous sections of the work is entitled "Proverbs of Hell." Blake, or his persona, strolls among the fires of Hell "delighted with the enjoyment of Genius, which to Angels looks like torment and insanity." The persona collects around seventy Proverbs of Hell to better understand "Infernal wisdom." Following are a few I have numbered:

1. Drive your cart and your plow over the bones of the dead.
2. He who desires but acts not, breeds pestilence.
3. Prudence is a rich, ugly old maid courted by Incapacity.
4. No bird soars too high, if he soars with his own wings.
5. Always be ready to speak your mind, and a base man will avoid you.
6. Everything possible to be believed is an image of truth.
7. The eagle never lost so much time as when he submitted to learn of the crow.
8. The weak in courage is strong in cunning.
9. Prayers plow not! Praises reap not!
10. Improvement makes straight roads; but the crooked roads without Improvement are the roads to Genius.

Blake knows a reader cringes at the mention of Hell, and so will be surprised and confused to find such wise and intriguing proverbs there. Moreover, he shocks the self-righteous reader into realizing that a denial of Hell is synonymous with a denial of such positive values as growth and renewed life symbolized by plowing (1, 2, 9); freedom exemplified by movement and flight (2, 4, 7); courage manifest in directness (2, 5, 8); and imagination and Genius inherent in nonconformity (4, 6, 10). The same reader is embarrassed to learn that these energies are contrary to revered, heavenly ones: sentimentality about death (1); restraint of feelings (2, 5); prudence (3); conformity (4, 6, 10); contemplation (3, 7, 9); shrewdness (8); praise (5, 9); and perfection (3, 10). Blake's devil's advice forces one to reconsider all priorities.

WORK OUT

Give some devil's advice to someone who you think deserves it: a politician, an employer, an organization or institution, a relative, or someone who has betrayed you. The important thing is too sniff out immoral, hidden motives as well as the illogic of what is not hidden in the person or group's argument. You may, but probably will not, need to slightly exaggerate these secret, ill motives and illogic. Instead of arguing against these grotesqueries or stupidities, "support" them by formalizing them into advice or a proposal. Allow the absurd to be showcased. Like Twain and Swift, keep a cool, steady voice, and without flinching, propose embarrassing desires and illogical solutions. Write as if you expect praise rather than contempt, but of course what you offer is worthy of contempt. What you praise or advise will be too outlandish for anyone to accuse you of really believing. Anyone who does deserves to be confused.

14
TALKING WORDS
Defining abstract concepts

Writers who try hard to define precisely and simply what a word or concept means often needlessly limit themselves. First of all, it is hard to beat the exactness of the dictionary. Columnist Jack Smith once demonstrated this point by asking readers of his newspaper column to define the word "chair." In the article he points to the tendency to say "it's something you sit on," a mistake since we sit on many things, including horses and stools. Smith asks how long it would take the reader to get "chair" down to Webster's dictionary's definiton: "A seat typically having four legs and a back for one person."

In this same article, Smith tries to meet a challenge by John Barclay, syndicated columnist of "Exploring Words," to define the word "time." Smith handles this challenge in several ways. First of all, he does something dictionaries cannot do. Instead of defining "time," he explains what time is not. Talking about what something is not turns out to be an important way of explaining what something is. As Smith points out, time cannot be "the space in which events take place" since this implies time can be stopped and started at a specific location, but we know time can also be something ongoing. The dictionary meaning relies heavily on the phrase "measurable period," but as Smith also explains, "period" is simply a substitute word for "time," and that anyway, a "period" is a specific time, but not time itself. In discussing what time is not, Smith realizes "our best dictionaries do not do well at defining the emotional content of our words. Time is a much more fascinating and intimidating idea than the dictionary definitions suggest ..."

Sometimes it is more interesting to define the less obvious implications of a word than those that are more usual or general. An anonymous writer in the "Talk of the Town" section of *The New Yorker* magazine, describes a conversation with Carolyn Lanchner, one of the curators at New York's Museum of Modern Art, in which Lanchner explains what the word "primitive" is by explaining one of its less explored meanings. The conversation is about the famous painter Henri Rousseau, who uses flat perspectives, smooth colors and textures, and simple shapes to form his wildlife subject matter. These are all elements that recall primitive art work. However, Lanchner points out that "primitive" is a dangerous word to apply to Rousseau: "'Was he the naive, self-taught painter who was mystified by everything? Or was he something of a mystifier himself — a man who managed to hold on to the freshness of childhood in a uniquely authentic, direct way?'"

In the rest of the article the interviewer emphasizes Lanchner's evidence that suggests Rousseau is an example of someone who meets the second, opposing definition of "primitive," someone who is a mystifier rather than someone who is mystified. The evidence includes Rousseau's remarks that his naivete was a style he had acquired by much labor; his admiration for technology; his experience with married life, children, and a practical profession as municipal toll collector; his direction of complex plays; his innovative backlighting of painted figures; his prolific career of an unquestioned hundred and ten pictures and a hundred and fifty that are of dubious authorship; his sometimes nightmarish subject matter that Picasso found both admirable and disturbing; his stylized concepts of depth; and his making a differentiation between his small paintings used as gifts to pay off small debts and his large paintings that he referred to as creations. These are hardly characteristics of the mystified, and mystified is the word usually thought of in connection with "primitive."

Another powerful way to define a word is to show how the meaning of a word is abused. In one article, sport's columnist Jim Murray defines what a "colorful" person is by demonstrating how the professional baseball business has corrupted the word "color." He points out that "to baseball, color historically has meant a whiskey-swilling, people-hating performer about whom poems are written, songs are sung. Color is getting sloshed in a bar and half killing a bar patron during a drunken argument." Murray goes on to give examples of such "colorful" people as Grover Cleveland Alexander who, staggering from the bullpen drunk in the 1926 World Series, struck out Tony Lazzeri with the bases loaded; Ty Cobb, who was legendary for his temper and hate; and Babe Ruth, whose belly came from bootleg booze and bathtub beer, not hotdogs and cokes. In contrast, Murray points to Dodger pitcher Steve Howe, who not only refuses to glamorize his drug addiction, but twice commits himself to a clinic at "great public embarrassment and humiliation." Not only is he refused the term "colorful" or having songs written about him, but the baseball business actually considers punishing him.

The journalist and fiction writer Ambrose Bierce's (1842-1914) devil's definitions also discuss words or concepts by showing how they are terms abused. Following are some examples: "DELIBERATION, n. The act of examining one's bread to determine which side it is buttered on." "DICTIONARY, n. A malevolent literary device for cramping the growth of a language and making it hard and inelastic. The dictionary, however is a most useful work." "HAPPINESS, n. An agreeable sensation arising from contemplating the misery of another." "HISTORY, n. An account mostly false, of events mostly unimportant, which are brought about by rulers mostly knaves, and soldiers mostly fools."

Defining a concept or word by explaining what it is not, how it is abused, and what it means in expected ways or under different circumstances, is the most complete way to define the full worth of a term and it is something a dictionary cannot do. For instance when the scientist, philosopher, essayist Francis Bacon (1561-1626) defines "suspicion," he explains what suspicions do (" ... dispose kings to tyranny, husbands to jealousy, wise men to irresolution and melancholy ... "); implies what suspicions are not ("... [something remedied] by procuring to know more ...); and demonstrates how suspicions have different meanings under different circumstances ("Suspicions that the mind of itself gathers, are but buzzes; but suspicions that are artifically nourished, and put into men's heads, by the tales and whispering of others, have stings.") Bacon elaborates on how to remedy suspicion, but even this has different results: confronting a suspected person with one's suspicion, clears those suspicions with the truth; but confronting a suspected base person with one's suspicions, simply makes that person untruthful.

Returning to Jack Smith's attempt to define time, one can see that he too not only talks about what "time" is not, but he defines what time means under different circumstances or considerations. He does this in a follow up article by acting as editor and having his readers do this for him. John Lindbron writes that "Time is just one damn thing after another;" Leo Ochs adds "Time is that stuff between paydays;" Jim Reed notices that "Time is what prevents everything from happening at once;" and Ed Mitchell offers "Time is something that wounds all heels." Dan Brennan sends in lines from Faulkner's *The Sound and the Fury:* "Father said man is the sum of his misfortunes. One day you'd think misfortune would get tired, but then time is your misfortune." Rabbi Alfred Wolf adds some thoughts on time

FULL-BLOODED STRATEGY

including "Time is meted out with complete equality to every living thing yet each of us uses the allotted share differently, sensing even the speed of passing time differently ... " and finally, the theologian Paul Tillich mentions that it is important to "'sanctify time,'" not "'to define it.'"

WORK OUT

Think of a word or concept that you feel is important to define for a small child, or is essential to define for someone to better understand what your business or profession involves, or is crucial for a lover or spouse to understand in order to better appreciate what you feel, think, or believe, or is important to define in order for someone else to better understand an artist, writer, area of science, or philosophy you are studying.

While defining the word or concept, remember it is important to go beyond a dictionary meaning, explaining what the word is not, as well as what it is in different contexts. Consider starting the definition with an ironic point of view whereby you explain how the definition of the word has been abused by those that ignore or take advantage of its meaning.

Words with definitions that might lead to interesting papers would include happiness, books, hands, paranoia, houses, babies, love, hate, education, cubism, computers, gods, contemporary, ancient, superficial, and original. If you define an animal, plant, chemical, physical law, or anything else that already has a fairly standardized, scientific definition, remember you are trying to define qualities that have an emotional fascination overlooked by these definitions. Again, consider what important things the scientific term is not, and what it becomes in different situations.

15
BLOOD FLOW
Revealing omnipresent forces

When the Judeo-Christian world thinks of something omnipresent, or existing everywhere, the first thing that comes to mind is God. Nothing seems more omnipresent than the Biblical God, not only because God is of the spiritual world, but because even among gods, none are as hard as God to pin down to a specific time or place. In his book, *Mimesis, The Representation of Reality in Western Literature,* Eric Auerbach explains how the writing of much of the Old Testament makes God even more mysterious than the Greek gods: unlike the Greek gods, God appears and reappears without warning; the reader is never sure of God's motives because He does not discuss them with other gods at

FULL-BLOODED STRATEGY

council, and the reader has no idea of what God does between episodes or where He has just been. In fact, there is generally a lack of physical details in the stories when God interacts with humans, so that God seems to be as much a part of a psychological drama as a physical one. By existing nowhere in particular, God exists everywhere.

But most worldly omnipresent phenomena can be placed in time and space. A writer communicating the prevalence of something has the task of dramatizing its magnitude so that the reader obtains a realistic sense of how overwhelming, how all-encompassing, it actually is. A good writer never over-estimates a reader's awareness of omnipresence. A good writer assumes that for most people omnipresent realities flow undetected, hidden below the skin of life's normal hustle and bustle. Two examples of all-encompassing forces that writers have successfully measured for readers include the black plague and prejudice against the handicapped.

Most of us know that the bubonic or black plague that ravaged Europe and parts of other continents in the Middle Ages constituted an overwhelming force of destruction. But in her book, *A Distant Mirror,* historical writer Barbara Tuchman uses two devices to further magnify the black death, detailing it beyond one's worst imaginings. First of all, she sprays the piece of writing with a consistent layer of geographical locations, dates, and population numbers. She guides us from one place to another, one time to another, one death count to another, so that all through the chapter we are forced to watch the disease reproduce and flow over the map of Europe. A typical entry mentions that "By January 1348 it (the plague) penetrated France via Marseille, and North Africa via Tunis. Shipborne along coasts and navigable rivers, it spread westward from Marseille through the ports of Languedoc to Spain and northward up the Rhone to Avignon, where it arrived in March ... In Paris, where the plague lasted through 1349, the reported death rate was 800 a day, in Pisa 500, in Vienna 500-600. The total death in Paris numbered 50,000 or half the population." Tuchman never holds up the flow of times, places, and death counts. The plague flows and flows; the map fills and overspills.

The second thing Tuchman does to dramatize the worldly predominance of the plague, is to show how widely and consistently the world goes awry, how wherever the black death touches, our normal expectations are also blackened. Being outside worldly expectations makes the plague seem especially powerful. For instance, the actual symptons of the disease seem unnatural, removed from the realm of normal pestilences: "... everything that issued from the body — breath, sweat, blood from the buboes and lungs, bloody urine, and blood-blackened excrement — smelled foul." The disease is so potent that to a French physician "it seemed as if one sick person could infect the whole world." At first, volunteers in Florence with red robes and hoods masking their faces except for their eyes, gather dead bodies, but they are soon outnumbered, forcing families to leave dead relatives outside doorways for dogs to drag away. Religious sacraments fall apart. Priests cannot keep up with the onslaught, die off themselves, and so laymen are given permission to offer last rites, and then women, and then finally the church issues orders that "'faith must suffice.'" One of the most incredible things that happens is that parents desert their children, and children abandon their parents. Absurd desperation reigns: villagers are seen dancing to musical instruments because "they believed that they could keep plague from entering 'by the jollity that is in us.'" By continuously blending such unexpected, abnormal details with a spray of cold, hard statistics, Tuchman successfully intensifies the scope of the black plague.

Prejudice towards the handicapped is a more subtle omnipresent force than the plague, but psychology and social work professors John Gliedman and William Roth in an article that became a chapter in their book, *The Unexpected Minority*, brilliantly expose such prejudice as being every bit as prevalent as the plague once was. Maybe more so.

Like Tuchman, they measure this dark presence by contrasting its results with what we expect to be true. They do this two ways, first by using an imaginary or "martian" point of view and secondly by a straight-on analysis of the subtle twists our minds make without our knowing it. First, the authors ask the reader to suppose an imaginary person from an advanced industrial society that "genuinely respected the needs and humanity of handicapped people" visited America. What would he take for granted or expect to find in a country where "roughly one-tenth of all children are handicapped, one-fifth of all adults are handicapped, and at least half of all able-bodied adults have a disabled spouse, child, parent, or close friend ..."?

Having an imaginary person consistently expect to find one condition but instead find the omnipresence of another, intensifies the revelation because it comes as a shock. For instance, this visiting person would "take for granted that a market of millions of children and tens of millions of adults would not be ignored," and so would expect to find cheap automobiles that could be safely driven by paraplegics, simple gadgets for domestic, everyday use, and industries, infused with the same vitality as the space industry, researching prosthetic devices.

He would expect to see handicapped people in books, television shows, cartoons, advertisements, factories, resorts, political action committees, and schoolrooms as the teacher or principal. The authors expand on each of these expectations, detailing each one and adding others. Our imaginary person expects to find all these things and so when he or she does not, the discrimination for the handicapped that is revealed instead, is even more disturbing. That part of the reader who identifies with the humane person is shocked too; the part of the reader that identifies with the world he finds instead, is terribly embarrassed.

In the rest of the essay, the authors switch to a second way to contrast what we expect to be true with reality, thereby showing the magnitude of this discrimination. They directly contrast our belief that we maintain an open minded attitude towards disabled people with the multitude of ways that a person's perception consistently twists or abnormally distorts when dealing with the handicapped world. For example, they point out that when a normal person notices someone else limping in the distance, they feel "pity, revulsion, or an interest in the unusual" and, as the limping person draws closer, revealing only a temporary cast, the normal person feels a sense of relief. When a person is perceived differently, that person is expected to be different. The perceptions of able-bodied people twist in some ways that are even more damaging than the mental distortions held by some racists. A racist demands that certain ethnic groups belong at the bottom of the social and economic ladder; an able-bodied person perceives the handicapped incapable of being on any ladder.

When an able bodied person does attach positive social significance to a disabled person, the able-bodied person does not realize how this is self-serving. For example, the person with sight layers exaggerated meanings over a person with an eyepatch. An older male with one is viewed as a person with a dark past, a will of special strength, "a capability for just enough brutality to add a trace of virile unpredictablity to the man;" but a seven-year-old girl with one evokes fear and pity. Even the able-bodied person's perceptions of famous disabled people such as Franklin D. Roosevelt, John Kennedy, Alexander the Great, Julius Caesar, Lord Byron, Alexander Pope, Elizabeth Barrett Browning, Milton, Beethoven, Nietzsche, Dostoevsky, Edison, or Freud become twisted in unexpected ways. Normal people mentally insist that this group is unique; that they *overcame* their handicap rather than simply carried on with life *despite* their handicap like other disabled people. Therefore, as famous people, these disabled end up not being able to improve the perception of the handicapped in general.

By contrasting what we think to be true with what really is, Gliedman and Roth convincingly demonstrate that the prevalence of a twisted mind set means that "to grow up handicapped in America is to grow up in a society that, because of its misreading of the significance of disability, is never entirely human in the way it treats the person within."

WORK OUT
Write about an attitude or philosophy that permeates a larger social group, geographical area, or time span than most people realize. Example topics might include an attitude about food

FULL-BLOODED STRATEGY

held by your family, a philosophy about sex during a specific time span in the history of rock and roll, a point of view held by the custodial staff about the professionals at your place of work, the expectations of people in positions of power, attitudes about youth held by clergy or teachers, the influence of an individual in a specific group, attitudes about humor in television commercials, aesthetic philosophy of gardeners in your neighborhood, or a feeling towards an historical event.

Or you may want to write on something of a more scientific nature. Everyone knows that worms are important to the soil, but Charles Darwin wrote an article on worms in 1881 that dramatized how greatly they influence all the earth's land masses. Like Tuchman with the black plague, he demonstrates how worms have an omnipresence and omnipotence beyond anyone's imagination. What else does? Consider flies, rain forests, rats, earthquakes, the impact of specific chemicals, instruments or machines.

You must have intimate knowledge of your subject and may need to do some research. Consider interviewing people in regard to their attitude or philosophy about a specific concern. Whatever you write on, be sure to demonstrate its large magnitude by including numerous or various examples where normalcy or what one would expect to be true is in effect upset by the omnipresent force you are writing about. Combine this strategy with at least one other: Tuchman's pinning the phenomena down to numerous times, places, and high frequency statistics; or Gliedman and Roth's using an imaginary person who expects a number of things to be true, which you list, but in fact is finally shocked to find the prevalence of an opposite force.

16
DOORS
Building ideas from openings

One way to build a successful piece of writing is to invest energy in its opening sentences. For the writer, thinking of an interesting, dramatic opening can sometimes crack enough light to develop an entire written work. An intriguing opening can spring a writer's imagination and argument, fueling more related thoughts or support material and possibly setting the tone of the entire work. The opening also is important to the reader. It opens up an unexpected room, drawing the reader into a world that he or she never realized before, and encouraging the reader to investigate eagerly the entire piece of writing.

FULL-BLOODED STRATEGY

Powerful openings need not be "formal introductions," a phrase which implies a beginning that is either a miniature summary of what the entire piece will cover, or a thesis statement of what the entire piece is going to prove. A good opening might include these elements, but an opening that can fast start and power an entire written piece must have more muscle than one made only of overview statements. Astonishing facts, literary allusions, metaphorical statements, and outrageous statements, are different kinds of doors that thrust open essays.

First Door

The advantage of opening with an astonishing fact does not need much explanation. An astonishing fact makes an argument or report specific and hard to ignore. The fact that according to FBI crime figures for 1981 there were 48 handgun murders in Japan, 52 in Canada, 42 in West Germany, 8 in Britain, and 11,522 in the United States, is not only going to give a writer much to think and write about, but will even pull some pro-gun slingers and political ostriches through the door and into the entire essay.

Other astonishing facts might include ones such as the following from a *Harper's Magazine* Index in 1984: 89% of the women in America, regardless of economic level, use deodorant, 75% of American men do, and at the same time, the average person in France uses two bars of soap a year; the average person has 7 to 8 sexual fantasies and 16 laughs daily; 10% of the Japanese have IQ's over 130, while only 2% of Americans do; 45% of Americans never read a book and only 13% of those who do not cannot read.

An overlooked advantage of the use of such facts is that it allows the writer a great deal of flexibility in determining what direction to take. For instance, suppose one started a paper with some facts about women writers from Tillie Olsen's article "Silences: When Writers Don't Write" such as her observation that most enduring women writers of the last century never married, and if they did, married late in their thirties, virtually always in the position to have servants. Such facts are interesting in themselves. Also, at this point the writer can move into one of many unexpected directions: an explanation of why these facts are true, or a discussion of women's creativity in general, or a report on women's social standing in the last century, or a comparison of creative women in the last century with this century, or reasons why creative people are neurotic perfectionists that need housekeepers, or speculation on why marital love and creativity, youth and creativity, or babies and writing, do not mix.

Second Door

Opening with a reference or allusion (not to be confused with illusion) to a well known past piece of writing, literary character, or specific literary incident, has its own advantages. First of all, the emotional and intellectual associations the reader has with the work alluded to, are quickly energized and lend their complexity to the present piece of writing. Secondly, works from the past that have proven their worth over time, such as the Greek myths, the Bible, or Shakespeare, carry weighty importance that automatically gets lent to the present piece.

Sigmund Freud went so far as to use Greek allusions as terminology to explain psychological forces. In his book *Freud and Man's Soul,* Bruno Bettelheim opens a chapter with an explanation of one of these allusions, an allusion to an allusion if you will: the myth of Eros and Psyche. Bettelheim points out that, "For readers who, like Freud, were steeped in the classic tradition, words such as 'eros' and 'erotic' called up Eros's charm and cunning and — perhaps more important — his deep love for Psyche, the soul, to whom Eros is wedded in everlasting love and devotion. For those familiar with this myth, it is impossible to think of Eros without being reminded at the same time of Psyche, and how she had at first been tricked into believing that Eros was disgusting, with the most tragic consequences." Using allusions to Greek myths, Freud was able to bring all the symbolic ramifications of those stories into his own psychological theories.

Of course there is the danger of using an allusion that the reader might not be familiar with. When that happens, the reader helps in slamming the door shut. As Bettelheim himself points out, not knowing the myths, a reader of Freud not only loses an understanding of what Freud was saying, but may invest those allusions with meanings Freud never intended. It is often important, then, to explain allusions. Doing so offers a good way to slip into a discussion of one's primary subject or material, and also prevents allusions from sounding like pretentious name-dropping. For instance, Bettelheim uses an explanation of the myth of Eros and Psyche as a basis to explain Freud's insights.

Popular fairy tales make for good allusions because everyone knows them. For instance, in an article for the *New York Times* entitled "Little Red Riding Hood Revisited," Russell Baker uses allusion to the tale beyond just his opening. He retells the whole story to make fun of modern day buzz words and jargon: Riding Hood took "foodstuffs" to grandmother, and "attained interface with an alleged perpetrator." In his book on transactional psychology entitled *What Do You Say After You Say Hello?*, Eric Berne uses the same story, reading it very literally to set up questions that probe for people's motivations: "What kind of mother sends a little girl into a forest where there are wolves? Why didn't her mother do it herself, or go along with LRRH?" Berne finally ends up with a script for real life riding hoods including someone who "doesn't often rescue people herself, but likes to arrange rescues ..."

Third Door

The readers of this book know the importance of metaphor as discussed in Part I, chapter four. But even when good use of metaphor becomes part of one's writing, the use of a strong metaphor to open a piece of writing, is often overlooked. Aside from capturing a reader's interest, a metaphor in the opening of a written work sets up a complex image full of ramifications and associations that may be explored throughout the entire piece of writing.

A good example of this is the title and opening of psychologist Bruno Bettelheim's essay "Joey: A 'Mechanical Boy.'" The title and opening sentence call Joey a mechanical boy. Bettelheim extends the metaphor in the following statement: "He funcioned as if by remote control, run by machines of his own powerfully creative fantasy." The metaphor is almost too apt. The essay is about a disturbed child who has absolved himself of all responsibility, including being responsible for bodily functions such as elimation and cleaning himself, and instead creates imaginary machinery to take care of it all for him. It is easy then for Betteleim to extend the metaphor of the machine: He borrows his imagery from the person he is writing about. Nonetheless, the strength of the opening metaphor is hard to ignore.

On the other hand, naturalist Edward Hoagland in his essay "The Courage of Turtles," opens with a metaphor that at first seems very inappropriate. He writes, "Turtles are a kind of bird with the governor turned low. With the same attitude or removal, they cock a glance at what is going on, as if they need only to fly away." The unexpectedness of the metaphor pushes the reader on but it also sets the direction for the rest of the essay. Birds are inspirational and symbolize a human's most positive desires. The essay is about the beauty of the turtle, how positive a creature it is compared to other animals, and how much it reflects the same mortal states we recognize in ourselves. Aside from coughing, burping, and producing "social judgments," they "pee in fear when they're first caught, but exercise both pluck and optimism in trying to escape." Comparing a turtle to a bird unlocks a new perspective on turtles and on life in general.

Fourth Door

Opening a written work with an outrageous statement is tricky and risky. It is one thing to be ironic, keeping a reader wondering whether the writer's shocking statements are straight or leg-pullers. (See "Devil's Advice.") It is another thing to make a statement that on a very literal level is blatantly outrageous. It is like opening a door in someone's face. An opening that stuns like an outrageous statement peaks curiosity. Readers do not like to be offended, but they cannot turn away from the excitement offense draws. In the following examples, such blows not only open the work, but become the controlling force throughout the work.

For instance, many years ago P. J. O'Rourke of Johns Hopkins University published an article in *National Lampoon* entitled "Foreigners Around the World." Each entry of the article is an outlandish description of a racial or national stereotype, including an outrageous description of racial characteristics, good points, and proper forms of address, obscene ones of course. The details are impossible to quote here, because as O'Rourke realized, every group must be included or else the piece becomes offensive. The article will offend some people regardless of what is done by the writer, but by including every conceivable group, O'Rourke makes *everyone* a grotesquerie and thereby demonstrates the absurdity of racial and national prejudice.

One of the most widely accepted masters of literal outrage was journalist, editor, and critic H.L. Mencken. The following is a typical opening for one of his essays: "All government, in its essence, is a conspiracy against the superior man: its one permanent object is to police him and cripple him. If it be aristocratic in organization, then it seeks to protect the man who is superior only in law against the man who is superior in fact; if it be democratic, then it seeks to protect the man who is inferior in every way against both." This statement from, "Le Contract Social," would offend anyone who idealizes their political system, but would not stop them from stomping through the door of Mencken's essay to see how he can support such an outrageous statement.

An even riskier essay by Mencken is "The Lure of Beauty." In the essay, Mencken goes after the human tendency to worship the body. Mencken does this by rendering the male and female bodies ridiculous. Even though he spends more time on women's bodies, his most potent statements clarify men's easy susceptibility to illusion. His opening statement is bound to outrage many men: "What men mistake for beauty in themselves is usually nothing save a certain hollow gaudiness, a revolting flashiness, the superficial splendor of a prancing animal." And later he makes mud pies out of the worship of women's bodies: "The female body, even at its best, is very defective in form; it has harsh curves and very clumsily distributed masses; compared to it the average milk-jug, or even cuspidor, is a thing of intelligent and gratifying design — in brief, an *object d'art.*"

Mencken's most potent statements clarify men's "herculean capacity for illusion." After explaining all the cosmetics and apparatus women use to keep men from seeing themselves as the "embalmer will see her," Mencken concludes that all "the tricks may be infantile and obvious, but in the face of so naive a spectator [men] the temptation to continue practicing them is irresistible."

Mencken enthusiasts would argue that his work is ethically justified because he goes after the sexual power tools in the human species, not the oppressed, or emotionally weak, or momentarily vulnerable individual. And like O'Rourke above, Mencken slaps all parties involved. Outrageous descriptions of a multi-million dollar fast food enterprise are more justifiable than going after the neighbor's kids' lemonade stand; going after male and female athletes in the locker room is more justifiable than taking on disabled people; outrageous statements about egotistical professors make more sense than outrageous statements about slow learners. But such advice is only generally true. Any group may have perverse or despotic elements that lend themselves to outrageous attack.

WORK OUT

Pick only one subject to write on. Pick three of the doors discussed above. Start three papers on your subject, using one of the three doors each time to complete the opening for each paper. Do not write more than fifteen typed lines per paper opening. Only after you have polished each opening, pick the most powerful one to use in a two to three page essay, letter, or article. In a few cases, combining two of your introductions may be effective.

FULL-BLOODED STRATEGY

For an alternative workout, instead of developing one of the three paragraphs into a complete written piece, write an essay explaining why you feel one of your openings is better than the others. Consider the opening's ability to capture the reader's attention, to stimulate your own imagination, to create a tone that you can sustain, and to influence or persuade the audience who would be reading your essay.

**17
SQUEEZE PLAY**
Asking for love

Sometimes good writing involves squeezing a lot of material into a small amount of written space. For instance, inter-office memos must say or imply a lot of information with a few words. Also, people squeeze play when they write short notes expressing love. Expressing one's love in writing is complicated at best, impossible at worst. Sometimes people turn to greeting cards for help, letting an anonymous writer run interference in love's dangerous world of vulnerability.

The important thing for a good writer to realize is that business and personal notes do not have to be boring or cliche throwaways. They can become explosive thought-capsules, sparking interest while they relay information. Imagine expressing the joys and dangers of starting a new phase in one's life in a short metaphorical note, to a friend or parent, that read like Gregory Corso's poem, "Last Night I Drove a Car":

> Last night I drove a car
>   not knowing how to drive
>   not owning a car
>
> I drove and knocked down
>   people I loved
>   ... went 120 through one town.
>
> I stopped at Hedgeville
>   and slept in the back seat
>   ... excited about my new life.

Corso's poem has the terseness of a note but is intriguing and thought provoking too because the second and third lines help clarify that the images are metaphorical. One of the most effective ways to learn how to say much with a little, an ability important to some extent in all writing, is to study poetry. A poet is willing to use words in any way imaginable that makes those words seem special and capable of saying a lot within a small, tight package of time and space. (Of course "small" is relevant to the time and space a message would ordinarily take to write, since some poems can go on for pages.)

Poetry fuses essay writing, a message made of complete and clear explanations, with secret coding, a message where unusual usage of words and phrases brings ambiguity to the forefront. Metaphor often helps in fusing these two verbal forces, and so becomes an essential part of poetry writing. (See Chapter 4 of Part I.)

It is impossible here to explore all the literary devices used by poets, but Andrew Marvel's forty-six line poem, "To His Coy Mistress" provides a good example of how a poet can compress a long, complex argument into a short amount of space.

In the first part of the poem, Marvel lavishes praise on his lover's beauty while he speculates that if one's time were infinite, he would savour his woman's beauty at an hyperbolically slow, but deserved, rate. Sexual contact could be put off indefinitely. If he "had world enough, and time" his "vegetable love should grow / Vaster than empires and more slow." He would use hundreds of years to gaze at the beauty of different parts of his lover's body, including "Two hundred to adore each breast," for that is what she deserves. With endless time, he concedes that her coyness would be no "crime."

The second stanza crashes against the first, using an original blend of objectivity and humor to uncover the rot that exists for reluctant, modest lovers:

> But at my back I always hear
> Time's winged chariot hurrying near;
> And yonder all before us lie
> Deserts of vast eternity.
> Thy beauty shall no more be found,
> Nor, in thy marble vault, shall sound,
> My echoing song; then worms shall try
> That long-perserved virginity,
> And your quaint honor turn to dust,
> And into ashes all my lust:
> The grave's a fine and private place,
> But none, I think, do there embrace.

The first two stanzas ready the lover for the third stanza, where Marvel explains his solution to the brevity of youth and asks his partner to melt with him in hot love as a way to challenge the gruesome realities of time:

> Now therefore, while the youthful hue
> Sits on thy skin like morning dew,
> And while thy willing soul transpires
> At every pore with instant fires,
> Now let us sport us while we may,
> And now, like amorous birds of prey,
> Rather at once our time devour
> Than languish in his slow-chapped* power.   *slow-jawed

> Let us roll all our strength and all
> Our sweetness up into one ball,
> And tear our pleasures with rough strife
> Through the iron gates of life:
> Thus, though we cannot make our sun
> Stand still, yet we will make him run.

The repetition of the word "now" helps heat the sexual impatience of the speaker. This kind of burning anxiety and concern for passing time also marks many rock songs over the past thirty years such as The Door's "Light My Fire," Fleetwood Mac's "Second Hand News," and Bruce Springsteen's "Dancing in the Dark." But horniness, personality, and appealing music aside, none of those songs have as seductive an argument as Marvel's poem of over three hundred years ago.

Love poetry may seem worlds away from a business memo but both have the potential to seem small and speak big. Learning to appreciate the compactness and richness of song lyrics and poems, you will have more fun and say more in any kind of note writing.

WORK OUT

Without a class in poetry writing or poetry appreciation, it would be asking too much to try to write an original poem. You might try writing some intriguing notes though. One way to do this, and at the same time learn something about poetry is to do the following. Go to the library or bookstore, check out a collection of poetry, and browse through it until you find a poet that excites or interests you. Now that you have a name, you might want to go to the card catalogue of the library and find a book of poems written by that person. If you have not had the opportunity to read much modern poetry, try to pick a writer whose poetry was published after 1920.

Now take one of the poems, keep its exact form, but change the words so that the poem has to do with a subject matter of your choice instead of the subject the poet has used. In other words, where the poet has one word in a line thus giving it special interest or importance, then you have only one word in that line; where the poet has a verb, you have a verb; where the poet has a metaphor, you must have a metaphor; and where the poet has a rhyme, you create one too. You may leave some of the words the same if they sound right with the other changes you are making.

The subject you change the poem to may be related to a business matter, a book you have read or work of art that has impressed you, a person who intrigues you, or a political situation that forever gnaws at you. You may want to turn the poem you have found into a love poem to someone you love, who loves you, or someone you wish would love you. Try to focus mostly on one issue having to do with love such as thoughtfulness, intimacy, sexual passion, jealousy, or a quality you do not like to see or are surprised to see in your lover.

No matter how you change the poem it will "work" because the poem's form has already been developed to make special sense out of the words it is using. Just be sure to stick to your subject. Do not worry about what you will end up with, simply have fun changing each line, each metaphor, each detail or image in the poem. When you are finished you will be surprised how carefully the poem's form has been crafted so that it makes your ideas, words, and images more special. You might want to send it to someone, but give credit to the original poet by including the phrase "after a poem by _____ (fill in with original author's name)" after your own title, which by the way, will have only as many words and kinds of words as the original title.

If you are not in the mood for romantic love, then look up Sylvia Plath's poem entitled "Daddy," which is easy to find in many literature anthologies and collections of twentieth century poetry. Then pretend you are Plath's "Daddy," and write a poem back to Plath keeping the form of her poem but changing the words as above.

18
FINGER POINT
Amplifying messages

The primary purpose of writing is to make something clear for somebody else to understand. Sometimes that is not enough. Sometimes it is necessary to make something so clear that it pushes itself out of the text, forcefully declaring its own importance. Usually we do not want to write so loudly. If the situation does not warrant it, the writer runs the risk of being obnoxious. But when such force is necessary, there are two basic positions to take: one is for the writer to symbolically raise his or her forefinger in the air; the other is for the writer to level his or her finger at the reader. Both kinds of finger points amplify messages.

FINGER RAISED

When making an oral declaration, or an extremely important demand, one occasionally would like to raise the forefinger in the air as if to mark one's words on the world. One way to approximate this emphatic gesture of striking the air in writing, is to follow every major idea with a list of supporting sentences that start with the same phrase. Each sentence becomes emphatic because the repetition of phrasing makes each sentence clear-cut, easily identified, and assertive. One of the best examples of finger-raised writing is the "American Declaration of Independence," written by Thomas Jefferson and others, and accepted in Congress on July 4, 1776.

The declaration starts off with a general statement of a universal problem without much finger pointing. In fact, except for the formality inherent in a sentence that opens with phrases and puts off the main subject and verb, the opening is humble and flexible. The writers assume that things do not stay the same, that sometimes "in the Course of human events" people are abused or disrespected and need to separate. The writers are interested in offering reasons for separation out of "respect to the opinions of mankind," rather than out of self-indulgence.

In the second part of the declaration, Jefferson and others outline their beliefs as to what a government should be and what in general constitutes a serious abuse by government. The finger raising begins. Phrases starting with the word "that," begin to drive the text: " ... that all men are created equal, that they are endowed by their Creator with certain unalienable Rights, that among these are Life, Liberty, and the pursuit of Happiness. That to secure these rights, Governments are instituted among Men, deriving their just powers from the consent of the governed. That whenever any Form of Government becomes destructive of these ends, it is the Right of the People to alter or to abolish it ..."

When the writers list the evidence that shows the King of Great Britain to have established "an absolute Tyranny over these States," they give eighteen "Facts," each one set off with a clearly raised finger in the form of an emphatic, repeated opening: "He

FULL-BLOODED STRATEGY

has dissolved Representative Houses repeatedly, for opposing with manly firmness his invasions on the rights of people," or "He has affected to render the Military independent of and superior to the Civil power," or "He has abdicated Government here by declaring us out of his Protection and waging War against us." When the writers want to list details under one of these points, they also maintain parallel structure, beginning each subpoint with "For" in listing all legislation the King has given assent to: "For quartering large bodies of armed troops among us," or "For transporting us beyond Seas to be tried for Pretended offences," or "For suspending our own Legislatures ..."

After this list, the declaration writers outline peaceful alternatives they have tried, again listing many of them with a common phrase. For instance, in regards to their British brethren, "We have warned ...," "We have reminded ...," and "We have appealed ..." The last part of the piece is a statement as to what is the States' only alternative, a declaration of independence and a call to action.

Finger raising is not just effective in political circles. In an article for *American Heritage* magazine entitled "Take My Wife — prithee," David Sherwood analyzes postings in Connecticut five years before the Declaration of Independence was written. These were notices written in the newspaper by husbands revoking their wives' right to make purchases and to register express dissent at their misbehavior. A key word these postings used to start every sentence or section was "whereas."

Here are some typical phrases Sherwood has collected from the men's postings: "Whereas Mary ... in years past conducted so towards me by taking weapons and threatening to kill me and many times wishing of me dead ...," and "Whereas Catherine ... [and] another man ... were often seen together in the night season; and about two years ago were found late in the night in a tight room, partly undressed, and the bed clothes turned down, and sundry times been seen in an unbecoming posture ..." The women pointed with "whereas" too. "Whereas he has ... in instances too many to be enumerated ... flung ashes upon me to smother me ... ," or "Whereas Richard Smith ... has represented me in a false and ungenerous light ... I think myself absolutely necessitated to ask the public how a woman ought to behave to a husband, who keeps himself (for the most part) intoxicated ten degrees below the level of a beast ..."

As newspaper headline lettering that glared the "whereas's" became smaller, and as petition for divorces encouraged women to take space in weekly papers, postings died out, but "whereas" is still a word used today as an effective finger striker, loudly calling attention to a reason behind a main point in legislative resolutions.

FINGER LEVELED

Finger raising, though, is not the only method to emphasize a sentence so that it leaps off the page. The other place to point a finger is right at the reader. To do this the writer writes in the second person, beginning sentences with the word "you" or leaving "you" out and implying the word "you" by using the verb form that is used with you. Writing in the second person amplifies a message into a command.

Some of the most thought-provoking commands are by Jesus reported by Matthew in the *New Testament*. Chapters 5 through 7 contain some of the richest, including: "You cannot serve God and mammon," "... do not throw your pearls before swine, lest they trample them under foot and turn to attack you," or "Enter by the narrow gate; for the gate is wide and the way is easy that leads to destructuion, and those who enter by it are many. For the gate is narrow and the way is hard, that leads to life, and those who find it are few." By pointing the finger at "you," or implying the word "you" before the opening verb, gatherers at the mount or the reader, are brought directly into a verbal piece and made responsible for what is demanded or directed.

A more recent example of pointing at the reader is demonstrated by Lewis Thomas, who has been chancellor of the Sloan-Kettering Cancer Center in New York City, and is a prolific writer.

His article "The Art of Teaching Science," was first given as a speech and later printed in the *New York Times*. He opens by mentioning how different factions of society and academia blame one another for what is wrong with the way science is being taught, and then he suggests that the scientific community itself might be largely to blame. The article is written in the first person ("I") for the first few paragraphs and then, as he outlines what should be done, Lewis literally uses or implies the word "you" in front of each suggestion.

For instance, after suggesting that all science education needs to be revamped from grade school to college, Lewis says, "Leave the fundamentals, the so-called basics, aside for a while, and concentrate the attention of all students on the things that are not known. You cannot possibly teach quantum mechanics without mathematics, to be sure, but you can describe the strangeness of the world opened up by quantum theory. Let it be known, early on, that there are deep mysteries and profound paradoxes ..." He says "Do not teach that biology is a useful perhaps profitable science; that can come later," "Teach ecology early on. Let it be understood that the earth's life is a system ... held in an almost unbelievably improbable state of regulated balance ...," and to "go easy ... on the promises sometimes freely offered by science."

Everytime Lewis points the finger at his reader, he holds the reader responsible for understanding and implementing his ideas. Near the end of the essay he returns to first person, mentioning that the problem with science is that the "fun" has gone out of it, that it has become an arena for embattled premed students just trying to get through, and that it has lost its aura of being the "high adventure that it really is ..." By concentrating on what is not known or what is mysterious in science, he feels students will become more interested in what is known and become interested in the mathematics necessary for probing further.

WORK OUT

In the 1800's the Woman's Suffrage Movement wrote a "Declaration of Sentiments" modeled precisely on the "Declaration of

Independence." Now it's your turn. To write your own declaration, look up the "Declaration of Independence" and try to follow at least half of it precisely, or design your own declaration that finger points by using the repetition of different phrases. You might want to look at some of Martin Luther King Junior's speeches. Write about any problem that you wish to take action on, first explaining the problem in general, then listing proof of the problem, then explaining what you have tried to do to solve the problem, and finally explaining the more extreme solution you feel you need to resort to. The problem may have to do with your love life, religious or philosophical point of view, family life, school or professional situation, or, if you wish to undercut the seriousness of your finger raising, the subject might be on something less serious, such as a problem with a pet, a car, a house, or a vacation.

Your other option is to write an essay about any of the above whereby you wish to hold the reader responsible for a change that will solve the problem. The beginning and end may be in first person ("I"), but the body of the paper, where you outline necessary changes and programs, must be written in the second person. Be sure your material is solid and important or leveling such a strong finger at the reader might seem out of place.

An even more creative option, is to give your reader directions on how to do something that is impossible to do. Directions are always given with an implied leveled finger. The impossibility of these directions will instantly turn them into a metaphorical finger point. The directions should be very detailed, giving the piece the feeling of being something that seems possible to do. Your goal here is to allow the directions to become a metaphor for something intangible and something more difficult to perceive. For an excellent example, see "Unchopping a Tree," by M.S. Merwin in his book entitled *The Miner's Pale Daughter*. The meticulousness, riskiness, and compromising necessary for putting a tree back together after it has been chopped to pieces, becomes symbolic of what it takes and what one gets when repairing a damaged relationship or one's own emotional hurt.

19
SINCERELY YOURS
Revealing truth in letters

Letter writing can be either the most personal or the most impersonal form of writing. For instance, many business letters lack personality and vitality. These traits are difficult to maintain when letters are directed either to a stranger or to such a wide range of people that they are written to no one at all.

The best letters, including the best business letters, will always be those that are directed to a small group of people or to a particular person. Letters are expected to be personal, by both the reader and the writer, because unlike books and published essays, letters are hidden in envelopes, to be opened only by the addressed individual. Letters imply intimacy. Although often abused or ignored, this intimacy makes letters one of the most powerful forms for written expression.

It is not surprising then that some novelists thought to build whole novels out of letters. Samuel Richardson was one of the first with his novel *Pamela* (1740) and especially with his more complicated novel *Clarissa Harlowe* (1748). Reading a slew of letters can become tiresome, but Richardson realized there were some advantages. He knew that following a plot solely through the letters of different characters, a reader would always know those characters with an intimacy so private that the book's author even seems excluded; his narrator having been banished as unnecessary. Aside from knowing reality through multiple points of view, reading different people's letters keeps a reader immersed in those characters' desires, doubts, indecisions, insights, and disappointments. These are the pulses that energize good letter writing in real life too.

One of the most famous letters ever written was a real letter by the writer Franz Kafka to his father in 1919. Many join the famous poet W.H. Auden in claiming that Kafka bears the same kind of relation to our age as Dante, Shakespeare, and Goethe bore to theirs. It is astonishing then to enter his private life by reading his sixty page letter to his father published in a bilingual edition by Schocken Books. Following are random excerpts:

Dearest Father:
You asked me recently why I maintain that I am afraid of you. As usual, I was unable to think of any answer to your question, partly for the very reason that I am afraid of you, and partly because an explanation of the grounds for this fear would mean going into far more details than I could even approximately keep in mind while talking.

. . .

From your armchair you ruled the world ... You were capable, for example, of running down the Czechs, and then the Germans, and then the Jews, and what is more, not only selectively but

FULL-BLOODED STRATEGY

in every respect, and finally nobody was left except yourself. For me you took on the enigmatic quality that all tyrants have whose rights are based on their person and not on reason.

. . .

It was only necessary to be happy about something or other, to be filled with the thought of it, to come home and speak of it, and the answer was an ironical sigh, a shaking of the head, a tapping of the table with one finger: "Is that all you're so worked up about?" or "I wish I had your worries!". . .

. . .

The main thing was that the bread should be cut straight. But it didn't matter that you did it with a knife dripping with gravy. One had to take care that no scraps fell on the floor. In the end it was under your chair that there were most scraps. At table one wasn't allowed to do anything but eat, but you cleaned and cut your fingernails, sharpened pencils, cleaned your ears with the toothpick. Please, Father, understand me rightly: these would in themselves have been utterly insignificant details, they only became depressing for me because you, the man who was tremendously the measure of all things for me, yourself did not keep the commandments you imposed on me.

. . .

Your extremely effective rhetorical methods in bringing me up, which never failed to work with me, were: abuse, threats, irony, spiteful laughter, and — oddly enough — self-pity.

. . .

You said something like this: "She probably put on a fancy blouse, something these Prague Jewesses are good at, and right away, of course, you decided to marry her... the next best girl. Isn't there anything else you can do? If you're frightened, I'll go with you to see her."

. . .

...marrying is barred to me because it is your very own domain. Sometimes I imagine the map of the world spread out and you stretched diagonally across it. And I feel as if I could consider living in only those regions that either are not covered by you or are not within your reach ... marriage is not among them.

WORK OUT

Kafka asked his mother to give the letter to his father. She never did. Write a letter to someone to whom you have something very important to say, but what you have to say involves a truth that would be so devastating to the receiver, that you could not send the letter.

The letter could be to anyone personally important to you: a family member, an employer or employee, a lover, a friend, someone dead or someone alive. Once you have actually written the letter and it has been evaluated, you may decide that you really should send the letter after all, or more likely, you will decide to burn it. Letter writing does not always need to result in sending a letter. A letter writer confronts a recipient with the same emotional intensity whether the would-be recipient actually receives the letter or not. Also the writer's deep, inner feelings are released and clarified in the letter writing process whether the letter is sent or not.

If you do not feel psychologically fit to write such a letter, then create a fictional character and have him or her write a letter that allows the reader to penetrate your character's subjective life. In his novel *Humphry Clinker* (1771), Tobias Smollett goes so far as to create a character, the maid Win Jenkins, whose very inarticulation provides insight into her deepest desires. Her misuse of words often suggests that she has carnal knowledge on her mind rather than suppositions and affections: "... but this is all suppository, dear girl; and I have sullenly promised to Mr. Clinker, that neither man, woman, nor child, shall no that arrow said a civil thing to me in the way of infection ..." Moses Herzog in Saul Bellow's novel, *Herzog* (1961) addresses imaginary letters to important officials, philosophers, and people out of his past, sometimes changing the addressee after writing the letter.

Imagine any kind of letter writer and recipient that you wish, but remember, good letters are intimate and detailed. Letters that are too general or too vague do not sound as if they were written to anyone.

20
MASKS
Eyeing new realities

By wearing a mask, a writer can transform familiar worlds into fresh ones, and at the same time make those discovered worlds come alive for a reader. To eye reality through a mask, a writer must imagine the mask as having its own mental and philosophical point of view, and own style of speaking. One advantage of using a mask while writing is that it disguises the writer, allowing the writer to say things that may normally be repressed or hidden in his or her own personality. Yet by writing in the first person singular (I), the masked writer maintains the intimacy inherent in a speaker talking directly to a reader. Disguised faces are creatively utilized by many groups: primitive tribes, protecting themselves for safe entrance into the world of their gods and demons; normally restrained people, masquerading at carnival time to wreak havoc and dance in the streets; or usually shy children, roaming their neighborhood on Holloween to demand treats.

Fiction writers have always talked through masks. A good example is the mask called Holden Caulfield worn by J. D. Salinger in his novel *Catcher in the Rye*. The first sentence of the novel uses a railroad-ramble structure coupled with slang ("lousy" and "crap") and lubricating phrases that say nothing but function to hold the reader's ear (italics). Together these elements paint the mask of the adolescent Holden speaking, a disguise laid over the face of Salinger, the adult writing: "*If you really want to hear about it,* the first thing you'll probably want to know is where I was born, and what my lousy childhood was like, and how my parents were occupied *and all* before they had me, and all that David Copperfield *kind of* crap, but I don't feel like going into it, *if you want to know the truth.*" Aside from releasing Salinger's creative powers, the mask intrigues the reader, pulling the reader into Holden's special vision of reality.

But starting a piece of writing through a special part of a writer's personality can involve more subtle masks. For instance, historical writers are usually expected to research the past thoroughly enough to be able to write about it as fact. But the editors of *American Heritage* magazine encouraged authors and scholars of history to comment on history through a different part of themselves. They asked them to write about the one scene or incident in American history that they would have liked to have personally witnessed and explain why. Most writers picked an event they were in some ways very familiar with and in other ways still curious and unsure about. Writing from this I-wish-I-were-there-to-find-out persona, resulted in writing that made history more real and intimate than when it is written as if it were totally factual.

For example, Oliver Jensen, one of the founders of *American Heritage,* wishes to return to the American Revolution at Lexington Green: "It might be possible to discern who actually fired first, a question argued ever since, but what interests me much more is the spirit of the moment, the attitude of the British officer, Major Pitcairn; of John Parker the militia captain; of the disciplined but ignorant Redcoats, of the farmers, and of onlookers. It's one thing to be part of history, but rather different, ordinary, horrible to be there and be hit." Jensen listens to the drums parade off with their emotional charge, a sound that he thinks might make drums "a bigger menace than the weapons."

The combination of knowing many things about the event and wishing to be there to know more, makes the event more real, more ambiguous, more a living thing. The same might be said of Emeritus Professor of English Leon Edel's response to the question. He wishes he could take a measuring tape to check on Thoreau's figures at Walden, "not to put down Henry David but simply to see what the distance was between the facts and his fancy. He had such a large fancy." Narrative historian, Walter Lord's response is another example. He finds the Golden Spike ceremony at Promontory Point, Utah, on May 10, 1869 to celebrate the first time the nation is linked coast to coast with a railway, a moment so full of promise that he chooses returning to it as a panacea to the darkness of present day realities.

Like a primitive tribesman entering a spiritual world that allows entrance only on special occasion, Lord steps into A.J. Russell's famous photograph of the celebration. More than the obvious captured truths, it is the unknown details that intrigue him: "I want to mix with that boisterous crowd of tracklayers, soldiers, dishwashers, gamblers, and strumpets. I want to listen to the 21st Infantry band thumping away. I want to watch the cowcatchers touch. I want to sample the bottle of champagne held out by the man standing on the Central Pacific's locomotive Jupiter. I want to know who the lady is in the exact center of the preliminary photograph, but who vanishes in the final, climactic shot. I want to know the identity of the one man in the picture who turned his back to the camera. Was he just inattentive, or was his likeness perhaps posted as "WANTED" in every post office in the West? I want to watch Leland Stanford swing his hammer — and miss the golden spike."

FULL-BLOODED STRATEGY 173

The responses to the *American Heritage* question illustrate that placing one's personality in another time period, and being allowed to wonder, is enough to release another part of the self. It offers another opportunity for putting on a new mask, playing a new role as writer, eyeing reality from a fresh point of view. Even more subtle parts of the self can be released by listening to different pieces of music while writing, allowing the music to influence the details and style of the piece. A writer might write on the same subject several times with radically different music playing each time and then compare the written works. One piece of music might result in creating a mask with its own voice that is more appropriate than another for the subject being written on.

A more dramatic way to masquerade is to become the object, animate or inanimate, which the writer wishes to analyze or discuss. For instance, by becoming one of characters in a specific painting, a portrait or crowd scene, a writer can explain details and their implications yet maintain the living vitality that is often forgotten when one critiques art work from a third person (he, she, it) point of view. For example, Walter Lord could have become one of the characters in the photograph mentioned above, using what he imagined to be that character's speaking style, but staying within the limits of what can actually be seen in the photograph in order to point out its details and indirectly analyze the photograph's worth. Often in children's books, authors become plants, refrigerators, or castles in order to explain the way those things function.

WORK OUT

One way to test the potential advantages of talking through different masks, is to take a scene in a published story with a substantial amount of dialogue and rewrite it three times, each time leaving everything exactly as it was first written except changing the main character to different people. Changing the main character means changing that character's responses both in content and style. For instance, in *Alice in Wonderland,* one could copy the scene with Alice and the Caterpillar, but take Alice out and have a well known politician respond to the Caterpillar one time, a well known singer the next, and a character from another novel respond the third time. The caterpillar's responses should stay exactly the same each time.

Another work out, would be to take a passage from a scene in a play by Shakespeare and change the scene at least two times, each time using characters that cover exactly the same content that Shakespeare's characters cover, but changing their personalities and language to those of a modern day group, such as teenage shopping mall girls, leaders of a motorcycle gang, British gentlemen, jive cats, remedial English teachers, computer hacks, debate champions, or corporate attorneys. Keep the dramatic situation the same, and match Shakespeare's lines line for line, metaphor for metaphor, but let these modern masks handle the situation.

21
NAY, IT IS. I KNOW NOT 'SEEMS.'
Revealing implicit truths

"Nay, it is. I know not 'seems'" is one of Hamlet's knife-like lines in Shakespeare's famous drama *Hamlet, Prince of Denmark*. The play dramatizes the struggle of a person trying desperately to cut through false appearances, through what seems to be true, to what really is true. Hamlet's struggle is every good writer's struggle. Truth is hard to find because self-deception, the intentional deception of others, and formulaic beliefs crust over truth's surface. These crusts make truth seem to be something it is not. Other times truth is not crusted over, but is ambiguous or mysterious and so seems impossible to perceive.

One way to prevent being overcome by "seems," or being dazzled by surface deceptions and complexities, is to carefully look at individual details after they have been cut away from the total situation being investigated. Since each detail is easier to concentrate on than the whole, there is less temptation to desperately jump to easy conclusions about the total truth than when one tries to understand that truth all at once. Therefore, creative thinkers do not immediately conclude the final truth about something until they have explored every detail's unique implications, significances, or meanings. Only then, when every detail has spoken for itself, does the writer come to a conclusion about the overall truth, a truth that perhaps the writer may not have expected.

It is tempting to believe that life is simple and that details do not have implied meanings because so much of life is carried on without the need to be aware. For instance, confronted by a picture of a baby taking a bath, a person of the Western world would not unleash his or her intellectual armies to free the implications of the details in the picture. The person would never consider that the image could imply anything but cleanliness. Nothing to uncover here, no ambiguity of meaning. But as the anthropologist Edward Hall points out in his article, "The Anthropology of Manner," women in India are visibly offended when shown such an image. They wonder "how people could be so inhuman as to bathe a child in stagnant (still) water." Babies and water imply rejuvenation but contained water has negative implications now skipped over in the Western mind. Hall is keenly aware that all manners have different implications, that the most common image cannot be taken for granted, and that makes him both an interesting social scientist and a good writer.

Manners are not the only things to be taken for granted. Even the simplest images of escape film or television shows have significances that are not usually given careful consideration. However, the well known anthologist and poet X.J. Kennedy takes nothing for granted in considering the American public's "love affair" with the gigantic gorilla King Kong. In his essay "Who Killed King Kong?," he explores several of the implications of Kong's physical or social nature. For instance, Kennedy speculates that Kong's being manlike reflects man's secret desire to "image himself a huge hairy howler against whom no other monster has a chance." In other paragraphs, Kennedy explores the significance of Kong wandering and smashing Third Avenue landscapes where audiences of 1933 wandered hungry, or hurling subways associated with work and drudgery. Kennedy realizes that these activities make Kong more likable to anyone victimized by ecomonics and the routine of the business world. Later in the essay, Kennedy considers the implications of Kong's physically dark image. The fact that Kong is dark might have special implications for oppressed blacks who could identify Kong with "a huge black powerful free spirit."

In trying to understand the audience's love affair with Kong, Kennedy also does not overlook the signficance of the fact that Kong is "a gentleman," always seeing that Faye is "safely parked," before thrashing a boa constrictor, and that such care is given "utterly without the hope of reward," since the two are so radically different in size. As such, Kong would appeal to any hopelessly yearning lover who is "impossible to discourage even though the love of his life can't lay eyes on him without shrieking murder."

By not overlooking any of these implications or associations, Kennedy can finally come to the truth about why audiences find King Kong so likable. It is a truth that is all encompassing, surrounding all the implications Kennedy has discussed: "It is not for us to bring a momentary stand still to the civilization in which we move. King Kong does this for us. And so we kill him again and again, in much-spliced celulloid, while the ape in us expires from day to day, obscure, in desperation."

Every important historical political event is of course loaded with significance. Historian Garrett Mattingly is a master at bringing such events alive by probing the implications of the details from which such events are made. What makes the first chapter of his book *The Armada* especially interesting, is that he writes about a queen who also knows every action or detail of one's life has implications, and she desires to exploit the significance of her own actions. The scene takes place in a large hall in 1587 where Mary Queen of Scotts is to be executed, having been run out of Scotland for possibly marrying her husband's murderer and now having plotted to murder her Protestant cousin, Elizabeth I, queen of England, whose protection Mary had enjoyed for sixteen years.

As Mattingly points out, Mary "learned how to dominate a scene," and she wishes to "play this last scene well" in order to convince the audience that she is a Catholic martyr. She knows that if her execution can imply her martyrdom, she will achieve two benefits: the political and military duel between Catholics and Protestants would continue in her behalf, and the "axe would cut off forever the burden of old mistakes, silence the whispered slanders" related to her personal life.

Aware that small details can have crucial significance, Mary makes the audience wait for three hours, to build up tension. As she enters, she rests one hand on an officer's sleeve, "walking as quietly, thought one pious soul, as if she were going to her prayers." Some think she smiles at the audience, but she gives her "grave inattention to her judges," raising herself above their political judgments. She thrusts a crucifix high, visible throughout the hall and raises her praying voice so that it slowly smothers the voice of her sentencer. She forgives all her enemies, a requisite move for a martyr. In what appears to be a final dramatic stroke, her ladies remove her black velvet cloak, revealing her crimson, "blood red" undergarments, a color associated with martyrdom.

But even after the "dull chunk of the axe," there is "one more ceremony to accomplish." Mattingly points out that it is customary for the executioner to exhibit the severed head and cry out "Long live the queen!" But as part of a final attempt to embarrass her enemies and create a situation that will forever imply her humility, Mary has pinned her kerchief to her stylish auburn wig so that both will come off in the executioner's hand. So now, as he raises the kerchief in the air, Mary's head pulls

FULL-BLOODED STRATEGY

off and rolls to the edge of the platform, "shrunken and withered and gray, with a sparse silver stubble on the small, shiny skull," a shriveled humiliation that could only invoke the pity given to a martyr.

Mary may have known how to create "seems," but as a writer, Mattingly knows to focus on her "seems," cut them away, and show us who Mary really was.

WORK OUT

Write about anything that seems so unique, so ambiguous, or so complicated that explaining its truth seems almost impossible. Follow the procedures outlined below.

Begin by writing notes listing all relevant, important details and then after each one, jot down your thoughts about that detail's implications or significance. Only after you have considered each detail on its own, should you begin to form a general conclusion about the truth. What you conclude may be complicated or simple, but you must feel that it is something that surrounds and takes into account all the smaller implications listed in your notes. You can start or end your paper with your conclusion, but the whole paper should be devoted to describing and explaining how all your details and their implications support that conclusion.

Before writing about the implications of details surrounding a political, social, historical, or economic event you may need to take time to research those details and then decide which ones should be given priority for consideration. If you feel that you do not have a great deal of knowledge and interest on a given subject in one of these areas, so that you do not need to do much research, then write on a work of art instead.

One of the advantages of writing about a work of art, such as a short story or painting, is that they are contained worlds, rich with complication, and requiring little, if any, research for exploring the meanings of their details. For instance, if you write about an important painting, all its details are contained within its frame, except its title. The title of a painting has implications that you will need to explore. And if the title makes the subject matter clear, indicating that the painting is about a specific Biblical, classical, or historical event, then the artist expects the viewer to know that event. It is the viewer's obligation to look that event up so that it is possible then to consider how the artist is interpreting that event.

What the viewer does not have to know though, to appreciate the painting, is the painting's significance in context of art history or in context of the painter's life (unless the painting is a self-portrait.) Knowing these things might help, but for this work out they should be ignored. The important thing is to consider implications of details having to do with the objects in the painting, such as people's faces, clothes, actions, and those details having to do with the setting, such as the man-made or natural landscape. Also consider the implications of the way lighting is used and the significance of colors and what they are used on. Consider the implications of specific textures, of arrangement of objects to each other and to the outside frame, and of the basic shapes of objects. Unless you have a great deal of background in art, avoid paintings that are totally abstract without any objects in them. However, paintings with identifiable abstract objects are fun to write on because the ways in which they are abstracted have implications.

If you write on a short story or film, consider the implications of the characters' actions and their dialogue. Details of the plot, special images, and the work's style itself, all have implications. In a short story "style" refers to all those issues discussed in Part I of this book. Film combines the elements of painting and story telling listed above.

22
REAL MAGIC
Snagging dreamy truths

All of us have experiences that are real but seem imagined, or have dreams that have the same impact on us as real experiences. These are delicate, fleeting realities that are difficult to communicate. Writing about either kind of experience requires a special blending of the realistic with the fantastic, a blending often found and easily perceived in the illustrations of children's picture books.

A good example of a picture book that blends the real with the unreal is written and illustrated by Chris Van Allsburg entitled *Jumanji*. The story is about a boy and girl who play a mysterious board game about jungle adventures. They heed its warning instruction that once started, the game is not over until one player reaches the Golden City. As the children play, the jungle obstacles that send players back spaces on the game board physically come true in the kids' house: chimps destroy the kitchen, torrential rains and volcanic smoke clog the living room, a lost guide squats on a doll house while he mumbles over a map, a python twists over the mantle clock. The situation is fantastic, but the animals and objects are not, especially since they are drawn in conte dust and pencil which gives them a soft, photographic reality. What makes the pictures dreamlike is not so much the appearance of jungle motifs running wild in the house, but the fact that every picture is shown from a point of view usually only possible in a dream. The viewer witnesses scenes looking up from just below armchair or table level, or even floor level, and sometimes looking down from a point half way up to the ceiling.

Writers trying to snag a fleeting reality that exists somewhere between dream and reality can also present it by viewing life from dreamlike positioning. Much of novelist, essayist Anais Nin's famous seven volume *The Diaries of Anais Nin* has examples of this dream viewing from different angles. For example, in her 1934-39 volume, she discovers Fez, Morocco. A frequent traveler, she senses that one "comes upon a city which is an image of one's inner cities," and for her "the layers of the city of Fez are like the layers and secrecies of the inner life." To Nin then, Fez is both very real, being a physically alive place; and very unreal, being a reflection of her subconscious aspirations.

To capture both, her mind transverses space quickly, viewing a scene from different angles, pulling together physical images that could only be brought together by the subconscious floating during a dream. Her mind gravitates to images that lend themselves to this kind of sweep, such as the streets and houses which are "intricately interwoven" by bridges and passageways, and by shadows from lattice work "that seem to be crossing within a house, you never know when you are out in a street or patio, or a passageway, as half of the houses are open on the street, you get lost immediately." The feeling of being lost contributes to the plausibility of a dreamlike sweep. And her vision even shock-cuts irrational violence into the architectual mosaic: "Mosques run into a merchant's home, shops into mosques, now you are under a trellised roof covered with rose vines, now walking in utter darkness through a tunnel, behind a donkey raw and bleeding from being beaten, and now you are on a bridge built by the Portuguese."

Often Nin will dream-sweep within the associations of a single image. A typical exploration is with birds on her visit to Puerto Vallarta, Mexico: "Then the birds, vivid, loud, vigorous, talkative, whistles, cries, gossip, clarinets, and flutes." She slides from adjectives describing birds, into nouns describing musical instruments that sound like birds, jolting moves in the conscious world, smooth glimpses in the dream world. Like in dreams, she feels passive even though she quickly covers large amounts of space, zooming from general observations like "color," to absurdly specific memories: "Passive drinking in of color, the cafes, the shops, people; and the thrill of looking into open homes, open windows, open doors. An old lady in a rocking chair. Photographs on the walls. Palm leaves from last year's ritual Easter. One room reminded me of Barcelona." Nin makes even larger mental splices, cutting from this passage to a nightmare from last night, then to fears about death. Nin creates magic by positioning herself outside single moments of time, sweeping from one unexpected angle of vision to another.

In his famous South American novel, *One Hundred Years of Solitude,* Gabriel Garcia Marquez does not make such radical, swift movements to blend the realistic with the fantastic. In fact, he does almost the opposite. He stays very still, keeping what he calls a "brick face," a flat, objective tone, as he describes dreamlike imagery happening in the midst of the everyday. In this sense he is like the artist John Tenniel, who in *Alice in Wonderland,* illustrates writer Lewis Carroll's fantastic images (Alice handing a dodo bird a thimble so that it can return it to her as a reward, a fish and frog footman in livery, a duchess with a gigantic manish face, a card queen and king) with fine ink-cross-hatched shadows. All beginning art students know that realistic shadowing makes even a drawing of a poorly proportioned object seem to be realistic. Likewise, the gradual, natural build up of shadow obtained through ink cross hatching can make the bizarre dream images of Carroll's book seem to be part of the real world.

Garcia Marquez's flat, objective tone works like Tenniel's realistic cross-hatching, rendering the fantastic credible. Writing about anything with a flat, brick face is like subjecting everything to realistic shadows: both devices make details seem realistic even if they are not. For instance, when Jose Arcadio Buendia, the patriarch of the novel's family, dies, Garcia Marquez uses the same flat tone to describe the magical flower-rain surrounding the death that he uses to describe the tedious work of a carpenter or street cleaner:

"A short time later, when the carpenter was taking measurements for the coffin, through the window they saw a light rain of tiny yellow flowers falling. They fell on the town all through the night in a silent storm, and they covered the roofs and blocked the doors and smothered the animals who slept outdoors. So many flowers fell from the sky that in the morning the streets were carpeted with a compact cushion and they had to clear them away with shovels and rakes so that the funeral procession could pass by."

For Garcia Marquez life is both real and magical, both very physical in the present and a vaporous legend for the future. Therefore, when he writes he feels completely at ease in mixing objective facts with images that can only happen in dreams. But the only way the two worlds mesh is through having both kinds of facts reported through Garcia Marquez's "brick face." He describes Jose Arcadio Buendia's great-granddaughter, Remedios the Beauty, and the events surrounding her, with the same bricktreated blend: "Men expert in the disturbances of love, experienced all over the world, stated that they had never suffered an anxiety similar to the one produced by the natural smell

FULL-BLOODED STRATEGY

of Remedios the Beauty. On the porch with the begonias, in the parlor, in any place in the house, it was possible to point out the exact place where she had been and the time that had passed since she had left it." When a roof tile-setter spies her naked in the bath and wants to soap her, she refuses, but mostly she is alarmed by the fact that he might fall through. When he discovers, as she dresses, that she wears nothing underneath as all had suspected, the proof is too much to bear. He removes more tiles despite her warning of how high up he is, and then he crashes to his death. But even amidst such dark humor, Garcia Marquez keeps a straight face to blend the mythical into the real: "The foreigners who heard the noise in the dining room and hastened to remove the body noticed the suffocating odor of Remedios the Beauty on his skin. It was so deep in his body that the cracks in his skull did not give off blood but an amber-colored oil that was impregnated with that secret perfume ..."

WORK OUT
Pick something to write about that seems unreal or something that seems as if it could have grown out of a dream. Typical subjects might include a foreign place you have traveled to, a garden or park you enjoy, a strange architectural interior, a shop or fashion show displaying the most up-todate styles, a social gathering with people you have not seen for a long time, a theatre or film experience and the environment you enter moments afterwards, traveling in what is for you a rare mode of transportation, using a new machine for the first time, meeting a group of unusual people, or eating in an unfamiliar ethnic restaurant.

Fold several pieces of paper length-wise. In the left column take as many notes as you can on factual details about your subject. It is best to take notes while you experience your subject or shortly after, otherwise rely on your memory. Write as many details as you can, including peoples' voice inflections, colors, shapes, shadows, lighting, tastes, smells, textures, light reflections, objects close and those at a distance, small objects and large ones, important details and insignificant ones.

Opposite the left column, write down something in the right column that you think would make an interesting symbol in a dream for half of the objects in the left column. This item in the right column can be a physical object, an unusual adjective, a piece of dialogue, a living thing, a title, someone from your past who haunts you, or parts of a real dream you have had. Write absolutely anything that reminds you of the detail on the left.

Only now are you ready to write about your experience. Basically you can use one of two tactics. Like Anais Nin, you can move through your material in the left column with dreamlike swiftness, sweeping together material in long sentences or quick, short diary-note sentences, while sometimes glimpsing at the most interesting associations you have made in the right column and sweeping them into your dreamy flow. Or, like Gabriel Garcia Marquez, you can write about your experience with a calm, objectivity and then, every so often, with the same "brickface," merge material, or ideas spawned by the material, from the right, dream column into you writing and report on them as if they were as real as your primary material from the left, real-life column.

23
FRAME UPS
Explaining with dialogue

One way to turn abstract ideas instantaneously back into flesh and blood realities, is to represent them in a dialogue between two real or make-believe people. Novelists and script writers have always let ideas and arguments live by being voiced through characters in discussion. There are also some philosophers, social critics, and other essayists who know that dialogue is a good way to transfuse life into ideas that might be whispered away if written about in straight prose. Authors discussed below who write from the lip include the ancient Greek philosopher Plato, the great British biographer James Boswell, and the syndicated social and political columnist Art Buchwald. It also includes many cartoonists, such as Trudeau, creator of *Doonesbury,* and Charles Schulz of *Peanuts.*

Cartoonists Schulz and Trudeau must be two of the most widely read chatter essayists of all time. They are essayists before they are visual artists, using their visual creativity to focus steady attention on their dialogue. For instance, there is very little movement within the frames of these comic strips. Both cartoonists view everything from a middle distance: no dramatic close-ups and long shots, or exaggerated perspectives with long shadows as there are in romance or super hero comic strips. Action and setting are cut off. Sometimes Trudeau even becomes more quiet. He repeats the same picture from the same angle in every frame such as continuous post-card views of the White House or a continuous side view of a character watching televison who shifts his beer can in one frame but otherwise remains unmoved.

And these men are serious essayists. Unlike most other syndicated strip cartoonists, Schulz and Trudeau are not always stripping a cute play on words or quick-smile semi-humor. Instead they give insight into the human condition. Schulz, when he is at his best, dramatizes keen observations about social behavior and mental attitudes by making fun of adult perspectives wrapped in the dialogue of kids whose mouths unwind more than their small tight bodies. Trudeau does even more. He moves into different social arenas, creates new characters, returns to old characters, and at any time within a single strip, can build layers of humor, simultaneously making fun of social, psychological, and political ideas.

Both cartoonists focus on dialogue very much in the same spirit that Plato does. Plato (427?-347 B.C.), in his important philosophical work *The Republic,* also maintains a very still background combined with total focus on dialogue to breathe real life into complex philosophical arguments that might lose vitality if written in straight prose. He does this by using the character of his teacher and friend, Socrates, as the primary speaker, and using an agreeable student as a fixed background prop. By responding positively to Socrates's probing questions, the pupil

FULL-BLOODED STRATEGY

is an excuse for Plato to continuously pull a book-full of dialogue from Socrates's mouth.

For instance, in a well known passage of the book referred to as "The Allegory of the Cave," Socrates sets up a hypothetical situation of a group of imprisoned people who never see reality, including themselves, in total light, but instead can only see shadows of themselves and other objects. At one point, Socrates speculates that if an enlightened person, a person who was shown the light and the way objects appear in that light, returned to the cave of shadows, he would fare poorly in a shadow-measuring contest against those who had never seen the light:

". . . would he not be ridiculous? Men would say of him that up he went and down he came without his eyes; and that it was better not even to think of ascending; and if any one tried to loose another and lead him up to the light, let them only catch the offender, and they would put him to death." "No question," the pupil verifies.

When Socrates brings his allegory together, explaining among other things, that "in the world of knowledge the idea of good appears last of all, and is seen only with an effort," the pupil cordially struggles through: "I agree, he said, as far as I am able to understand you." All the philosophical complexities of Plato's entire book are brought alive through this tension between a questioning complex man and a simple, attentive pupil.

James Boswell's biography about Johnson, Boswell's friend and well known eighteenth-century moralist and writer, entitled *The Life of Samuel Johnson,* primarily focuses on dialogue between the two men. But Boswell plays a much more active part than Socrates' pupil. First of all, before he even starts to write, the twenty-two year old Boswell deliberately manipulates his older friend's life, dragging him off to a rugged visit in the Hebrides, arranging for him to dine with notorious people or ones he knows Johnson dislikes, and asking a range of questions having to do with both the mundane and the philosophically important. all for the purpose of cultivating more telling dialogue.

Unlike the character of Socrates, Johnson answers questions rather than raises them. Boswell's questions become the device to pull a huge book full of witty dialogue out of Johnson: "...I asked him what he thought was best to teach them [children] first. *Johnson*. 'Sir, it is no matter what you teach them first, any more than what leg you shall put into your breeches first. Sir, you may stand disputing which is best to put in first, but in the mean time your breech is bare. Sir, while you are considering which of two things you should teach your child first, another boy has learnt them both.'" When Boswell and dinner guests wonder if drinking improves conversation and benevolence, Johnson disagrees: "'No, Sir: before dinner men meet with great inequality of understanding; and those who are conscious of their inferiority, have the modesty not to talk. When they have drunk wine, every man feels himself happy, and loses that modesty, and grows impudent and vociferous: but he is not improved; he is only not sensible of his defects.'"

One of the values of Boswell's book is that it covers all aspects of eighteenth-century life in England, including its prejudices. When Boswell comments that he heard a woman preach at a Quaker ceremony, Johnson responds with prejudice, but with great metaphoric wit: "*Johnson*. 'Sir, a woman's preaching is like a dog's walking on his hinder legs. It is not done well; but you are surprized to find it done at all.'" Many of us would be offended today by such a remark about women, but nonetheless, it is this kind of witty dialogue that makes this book about the intellectual, moral, and social history of England in the eighteenth-century live in a way that it would not if it were written in straight prose.

A more contemporary dialogue essayist is syndicated columnist Art Buchwald. For years, most of his short columns have been ironic dialogues used to comment on everything from politics to fashions to social mentality. To make his points he has had make-believe chit chats with young future presidents, has opened a gym locker to find a press correspondent explaining why he is hiding out from the president, has rewritten film script dialogue such as the western *High Noon* with allusion to

FULL-BLOODED STRATEGY

political gun slingers, has put opposing political figures together in a rescue boat, has interviewed Congressman Michael O'Lobby from the state of Indignation, has warned his son and other leg men about designer treatment of women's stockings, has surveyed children's attitudes on school prayer to find out that many like it as a way to do better on tests, has documented the conversation of a husband and wife having an affair with each other only to return home to their boring selves, and has imagined a conversation between early Pilgrims who decide growing beautiful lawns is more improtant than growing produce.

A typical dialogue is from a column entitled "Fathers for Moral America." Reacting to Mothers for a Moral America who try to put a film on television depicting examples of "moral decay," the fathers decide to help out. When Art asks a spokesman of Fathers for Moral America what they do, he responds, "We have a screening room in the back where we show dirty movies every two hours. We want to alert the fathers of America to the terrible degeneration that is going on in the United States. The response has been heartwarming. Ever since we started the screenings, there hasn't been an empty seat in the house." When Art asks what the reaction is, the spokesman replies, "The majority of them leave shocked that things like this could be happening in this country, and many come back a second time because they can't believe it." Among other things, Art finds out that when the men are shown the latest in topless swim wear they are so shocked they cannot eat, that the reading room that displays examples of salacious books is one of "most popular exhibits," and "alarmed fathers" man telephones to let other fathers know what to watch for at local theaters. Art becomes emotionally impressed and wants to know when the next film begins. In essence, Art Buchwald has created a cartoon strip, with himself included inside the frames, to both make a statement about who he feels moral decency types really are and to depict the absurdity of censorship.

WORK OUT

Make up a rough draft of a thirty frame cartoon strip with stick figures if you cannot draw. When you are done, try to condense the dialgoue and reduce the strip to ten frames. Then do it this again, reducing the strip to four or five frames. All that is important is the dialogue. You must start with more frames than you will need or you risk leaving out important details or oversimplifying your point. Create two more strips using this procedure so that you have three good strips that all have to do with the same issue. Assume that if they were real cartoon strips they would run on three consecutive days in the newspaper.

As with the Johnson and Buchwald examples, you may be a questioning interviewer in the frames, or you may use another character to talk with or question the primary character in the strip. This primary character can be anyone in any kind of situation that lends itself to your making a specific social, psychological, historical, political, scientific or philosophical point.

For instance, your characters could be a famous scientist or literary figure applying to graduate school, your parents arguing with each other about your spouse or lover, a political figure talking to you about a class you are both taking together, a fashion designer discussing a clothing problem with a well known celebrity, a group of philosophers or characters from films or novels meeting on a television talk show. The possiblities are endless. Try to use the style of language your characters use: the same kinds of words and sentence lengths.

Every bit of dialogue must be revealing and must count since you only have four or ten frames to make your point. Your strip may be humorous like Buchwald's and the cartoonists, or follow a serious argument like Plato's, or be moralistic and witty like Boswell's. In any case you will make a point that lives in a way impossible to create with straight argumentative prose.

24
DUST IN THE LIBRARY
Avoiding dead research papers

Most people enjoy doing research papers in their heads, almost without knowing they are doing them. A woman has a house plant and cannot decide where she should put it to get enough light. She calls the nursery where she bought it, talks to a friend who has a similar plant, and maybe consults one or two plant books. All these sources blend in the person's brain, pros and cons are balanced, and a decision is made as to where to put the plant. The woman watches to see how the plant is doing, and this experiment is meshed with the previous material about the plant. Finally an even better decision is made as to where to put the plant.

Research is the integrating of material from outside sources or experiments until there is enough mixed material to harden into a decision about the issue at hand. Most people enjoy doing research when they are interested in what they are finding out and when they do their research in their skull without having to write it out. Everytime we visit bike shops and read consumer magazines to look for a better bike, or call travel agents and read vacation books to make sure a trip looks promising, we are doing research. A teenager does not mind at all doing research on someone of the opposite sex in whom he or she is especially interested. The research can involve several live interviews and phone calls, plus close "field" observation of the person in question. The researching teenager does not mind spending hours of time scrambling sources together to make a decision about the other person. The process happens almost unconsciously, but it is still research, even if the support material gets scorched by passion.

Several professions require cooler research, and require it to be written out and documented. Attorneys, some business executives, and students are included in this group. Still, researching can happen almost automatically without any attention paid to leg work, as long as a person cares about his subject. But writing this material down, integrating it, and documenting it takes extra time and thought, so it can be especially deadly if the writer is not vitally interested in his subject. Try to avoid this situation. There are enough other problems that can turn interest in writing a research paper into dust. Following are ways to avoid them.

First, when you go to the library to look up material, and find that most of what you read is difficult to understand or monotonous to read, stop and ask yourself whether it is the content that is crumbling your comprehension, or whether it is the writer's style. Much of the written world is not in full-brain style. Look for pieces that are. Or at the very least, realize that you can take what dead-head, but knowledgeable writers write, and full-brain their material, rewriting it into your paper in your own style. Just be sure to footnote. If you combine three authors' ideas together in a railroad ramble sentence, footnote every sec-

FULL-BLOODED STRATEGY

tion of the sentence that has someone else's ideas. Most people think that footnotes are used only for word for word, direct quotes from other writers, but quotation marks (") signal that. Footnotes are for giving credit to another author for his or her ideas, regardless of whether the idea is in that writer's words, or your words.

Secondly, do not worry about memorizing proper forms of documentation. There are several good sources for understanding the mechanics of doing a research paper, including Barron's *10 Steps to Writing the Research Paper* or the Modern Language Association style book. Most give the proper footnote and bibliography form for every kind of source from scholarly books to bathroom graffiti. They also give information on using the library, but asking librarians questions and walking the mazes of the library are the best ways to discover how to use the library.

When you take notes, do not worry about how all your information is going to eventually fit together. Barron's book listed above discusses methods for putting notes on notecards instead of on large pieces of notebook paper. Putting each idea from a writer's work on its own separate card frees you to psychologically shatter that source into information bits that can be more easily pieced together with those from other sources. When notes from one source are kept together on one piece of notebook paper, there is a greater tendency to keep all the details from that writer together in your paper, instead of mentally and physically shuffling that writer's information together with the other material you collect.

Finally, and most importantly, realize that research papers are no more important than any other kind of paper mentioned in this book. With this perspective you will be more relaxed and more willing to model the paper with any combination of strategies discussed in Part II of this book, or any another approach that is full-blooded in spirit.

For instance, Geoffrey Bibby of the Denmark Historical Museum wrote a piece entitled "The Body in the Bog." This was a carefully researched piece that explained why Bibby believed a naked male body, preserved in a peat bog from over 1500 years ago, was killed. To decide, he pulled together a wide range of sources: a professor of forensic medicine, who figured out that the male died by having his throat slit; botanists, who determined how the body was buried by counting infinitesimal grains of pollen; radio-carbon data that dated the death around A.D. 310; historical records that connected this body with those found at much earlier dates; archaeologists of Danish prehistory, who clarified early notions of beliefs in afterlives; the Roman historian, Tacitus, whose account of German tribes in A.D. 98 distinguished the man's probable tribe by its common worship of Nerthus, or Mother Earth, a goddess that demanded human sacrifice for peace; a study of European spring festivals whose characteristics linked with Mother Earth celebrations through notions of fertility; and finally the food contents found in the stomach itself, grains associated with winter storage and with no trace of the plants or fruits of summer, placing the murder in spring.

Bibby uses a wide range of sources and his own cleverness to interconnect them, thereby establishing that the murder was probably committed for religious reasons. Just as important, Bibby keeps the reader interested in his picking and shoveling into the past by creating suspense in the present. For instance, instead of setting the problem in the archaeological past, one of his opening passages gives the hunt the urgent presence of a detective mystery: "My part in the story began on Monday, April 28, 1952, when I arrived at the Prehistoric Museum of Aarhus, in mid-Denmark, to find a dead body on the floor of my office." Then later, "So the man from Grauballe had had his throat cut, and we had a murder mystery on our hands." And much later, "It is clear, I think, that we have a case of mass murder." The whole article is written with the tension of a murder mystery, almost a strip tease where the reader anxiously awaits each new detail that might solve the case. This makes the article full-blooded. No dust here.

Researched papers can also be meaningful even when they are "false." The great Argentine writer, Jorge Luis Borges, often interjects his fictions and critical essays with documented research that is made up. Borges does this for many reasons. One is to underscore his attraction to different perspectives on reality and demonstrate that he also does not believe that anything is absolutely true, by making all sources of information suspect. Sometimes he uses documentation to help create the tone of a scrupulous scholar in order to make metaphysical and metaphorical truths believable. And other times he uses "researched" details to simply create another fork in the road, another corridor within a labyrinth of corridors, because for Borges everything in life has infinite dimensions and infinite possibilities. Exploring Borges's specific uses of research here would take too much space, but his collection entitled *Labyrinths: Selected Stories and Other Writings,* has numerous examples.

In 1917, the great American journalist and critic, H.L. Mencken, wrote what was later titled "The Bathtub Hoax" in the *Chicago Tribune,* a well faked, but documented, history of the bathtub to commemorate its "neglected anniversary." The essay is complete with specific, "researched" details such as "the fact" that "the first American bathtub was installed and dedicated so recently as December 20, 1842 ...," and "in England in 1828 by Lord John Russell" where "its use was yet confined to a small class of enthusiasts." These are subtle slaps at humanity: Could we really have waited so long to formalize bathing? It sounds like it. The spoof goes on to dramatize a conflict, every blow of it documented with dates and names and places, between some Cincinnatians, that enjoy taking the plunge, and others, including those who see the bathtub as an "epicurean and obnoxious toy from England, designed to corrupt the democratic simplicity of the republic," and the medical profession who are "quoted" as saying the tub is an inviter of "zymotic diseases." Some time later, Mencken published an article explaining the history as a spoof; digging up the real history of the tub would have been a "dreadful job." He claimed that he wanted to demonstrate that people enjoy lies as long as they are agreeable, complete with heroes and villains. "Researched" material is crucial, but don't always trust it. There might be a Mencken on the other side.

WORK OUT

Write a research paper or write a spoof of one. If you write a research paper, write about something you are truly interested in but want to know more about: Which carburetor system is better for your car?; Which city in your state has the best vacation possibilites?; Will Africa be able to solve its hunger problems?; Is a cabbage patch doll better for a girl to own than a Barbie doll?; Which of two regional architects is best for building a specific new campus facility?; Would you have enjoyed your birthday on its true date but in a specific year before 1960? The last topic provides a meaningful way to learn about the history of food, politics, clothing, interior decorating, ideas or religions, and technology. With any of the topics, be sure to use full-brain style and a writing strategy that is full-blooded in spirit, including any one listed in this book.

If you write a short, three to five page typed paper, develop only one point, using only material relevant to that point, but organized under different categories. Consult one of the research books mentioned above. Do not let definitions or background information get in the way of your argument. If you need to include such material, consider putting it in footnotes. Footnotes can be used for this purpose as well as for documenting material.

If you write a spoof, you will still need to study a typical research paper in order to make your paper look and sound like one. Deaden your use of full-brain style. Use your burlesque to make fun of related issues on the subject you have picked to write about; do not use it to merely make fun of research papers. You will need to make up interesting sounding material you pretend to have looked at. Every topic has possibilities: the reasons for the emergence of a particular field of study, a proposal for a new kind of school for future teachers or doctors, why one sport is better than another, or the influences of a fast food franchise on particular gourmet restaurants. Have fun, but stay detailed.

25
BILLY FAULKNER
Inventing full-blooded strategy

Full-blooded strategies are learning experiences. Full-blooded strategies are also resources for future writing, chapters to which you can return for writing formats that will successfully organize and dramatize your written thoughts for your educational pursuits, professional endeavors, and personal life.

But perhaps even more importantly, the strategies lead you through a small part of the endless creative-spirit maze, a maze that is complicated by the vast possibilities of ways to create pieces of writing. It is a maze that many are afraid to enter. However, now that you feel comfortable with most of the full-blooded strategies presented in this book, you will begin to realize that the maze can be one to enjoy.

Part of that enjoyment means realizing that you can create good written pieces by overlapping and combining strategies discussed in this book. The other part of that enjoyment involves taking an interest in all good writers, taking delight in their uniqueness and appreciating their differences. If you do this, the twists and turns that those writers add to the maze will not be threatening. By studying those writers you will eventually create your own full-blooded strategies. Even the best fiction and prose writers of this century, like William Faulkner, will yield some of their secrets if you search for them.

There are many forces that can spoil your attempt to create original full-blooded strategies. One is simply to become panicked by the endlessness of the maze, desperately seeking its end with the hope that it might yield an an absolute answer, an ideal, one correct way to write about everything. But there is none. Once you no longer enjoy entering the unexpected turns and following the unfamiliar paths of the maze, your creative spirit will fade.

Studies done by psychology professor Teresa Amabile of Brandeis University also confirm that a need for an absolute answer in terms of an extrinsic reward can spoil creativity. Creativity is hampered when one does "something in order to get something back, like money, a gold star from the teacher, meeting a deadline," as opposed to "doing something primarily for its own sake, because it is fun." Professor Amabile stresses Albert Einstein's statement reflecting his fear that most educational systems encourage use of extrinsic rewards and punishments as a means of teaching. He felt that it was "a very grave mistake to think that the enjoyment of seeing and searching can be promoted by means of coercion and a sense of duty."

In fact, all that the full-blooded strategies in this book can do for you is to open the first few doors of the maze. Your decision to travel through it must come from your own longing and motivation.

FULL-BLOODED STRATEGY

WORK OUT

Write on any subject of your choice by combining two of the full-blooded strategies in this book. For instance combine the strategy of "Double Exposures" with those of "Dust in the Library," or "Real Magic" with "Blood Flow," or "Frame Ups" with "Talking Words," or "Sliced Pie" with "Devil's Advice," or "Splitting the Second" with "Ugly Giants." There are at least four-hundred combinations.

A second option is to read chapters from different books, or essays from the many college readers found in college book stores, or articles from magazines and newspapers. Pick two or three of the best ones and write an essay explaining under what full-blooded strategies in this book you would put them. Explain why you think the pieces you found are as good, worse, or better than the ones in this book.

A third option for a work out is to read a chapter from a well written book or an intriguing article from a magazine. After reading it several times, analyze the piece as if you were going to include it in this book. If appropriate, point out characteristics the writer's strategy shares with other writers you have read. Most importantly, discuss what makes the writer's strategy unique and explain its organizational and psychological advantages. Then design a work out that you think would help others to test and appreciate the full-blooded strategy you have discussed. Be very specific in your explanation and give examples of topics that might best be subjected to the strategy. Think of an intriguing title for your piece and a subtitle that reflects the strategy's broad applicability.

NOTES

PART I
SMOOTHING THE FLOW
The Brothers Grimm, "Little Red-Cap," *The Complete Grimm's Fairy Tales*, (New York: Pantheon Books, 1980), p. 139.

Ernest Hemingway, *The Sun Also Rises*, (New York: Charles Scribner's Sons, c. 1954), p.25.

Jim Quinn, "The Joys of Watergate," *American Tongue and Cheek*, (New York: Penquin Books, 1982), p.76.

Moiara Johnston, "The Chip," *National Geographic Magazine*, (October, 1982), p.421.

Annie Dillard, "Fecundity," *Pilgrim at Tinker Creek*, (New York: Harpers Magazine Press, 1974), p.161.

Joan Didion, "In Bed," *The White Album*, (New York: Simon & Schuster, c.1979), p.169.

Edward Stern, *Perscriptive Drugs and Their Side Effects*, (New York: Grosset & Dunlap, 1977), p.39.

Manny Farber and Pat Patterson, "Fassbinder," *Film Comment*, November-December, 1975, pp. 5-7.

Jane Austen, *Pride and Prejudice*, (Great Britain: Penquin Books Ltd., 1982), p. 174.

Norman Mailer, *Of a Fire on the Moon*, (Boston: Little, Brown, & Co., 1970), p.373-374.

Cameron McKinley, "Adventures in Texture and Tone," *Architectural Digest*, (June 1983), pp. 97-103.

William Shakespeare, "Hamlet Prince of Denmark," *William Shakespeare: The Complete Works*, (New York: Viking Press, 1979), Act I, scene v., p.941.

William Faulkner, *The Sound and the Fury*, (New York: Vintage Books, c.1946), p. 165.

Paul G. Hewitt, *Conceptual Physics*, 4th ed. (Boston: Little, Brown, & Co., 1981).

Lewis Thomas, "The Tucson Zoo," *The Medusa and the Snail: More Notes of a Biology Watcher*, (New York: Viking Press, 1979), p.10.

Harold Pinter, *The Homecoming*, (New York: The Grove Press, 1982), p. 31.

James Walcott, *New York Magazine*, "A Priest Called Ralph," (March 28, 1983), p. 88. Includes a review of "We're Dancin."

Arnold Hauser, "The Empire and the End of the Ancient World," *The Social History of Art*, (New York: Vintage Books, c.1951), p. 109.

Flannery O'Conner, "Greenleaf," *Everything That Rises Must Converge*, (New York: Farrar, Straus and Giroux, 1977), p. 53.

NOTES Continued

PART I SMOOTHING THE FLOW Continued
Ernest Becker, *The Denial of Death*, (New York: Free Press, 1975), p.263.

Jonathan Swift, *Gulliver's Travels*, (Great Britain: Penquin Books Ltd., 1979), p. 158.

GIVING PAUSE
Bonnie Prudden, *Your Baby Can Swim*, (New York: Reader's Digest Press, 1974), p. 109.

Geoffrey Chaucer, "The Pardoner's Prologue," *The Canterbury Tales*, (Great Britain: Penquin Books Ltd., 1977), p.262.

Roger Angell, "On the Ball," *Five Seasons, a Baseball Companion*, (New York: Simon & Schuster, c.1977), p. 12.

Joseph Heller, *Catch 22*, (New York: Dell Publishing Co., 1980), p. 450.

Barbara Tuchman, "This is the End of the World: The Black Death", *Distant Mirror: The Calamitous 14th Century*, (New York: Alfred A. Knopf, 1978), p.100.

Joan Didion, "Los Angeles Notebook," *Slouching Towards Bethlehem*, (New York: Farrar, Staus, & Giroux, 1968), p.217.

Robert Coover, "The Gingerbread House," *Pricksongs & Descants*, (New York: Plume Books, 1970), p. 63.

Apple IIc: An Interactive Owner's Guide, (Cupertino: Apple Computer, Inc., 1983). p. xii.

Alice Quiros and Barbara L. Young, *The World of Cactus & Succulents and Other Water-Thrifty Plants*, (San Francisco: Ortho Books, 1977), p. 65.

Annie Dillard, "Heaven & Earth in Jest," *Pilgrim at Tinker Creek*, (New York: Harpers Magazine Press, 1974), p.7.

Natachee Scott Momaday, *House Made of Dawn*, (New York: Perennial Library, 1977), pp. 20-21.

Margaret Mead and Rhoda Metraux, "New Superstitions and Old," *A Way of Seeing,* (New York: McCall Publishing Co., 1970), p.264.

Lewis Mumford, "Compensations and Revisions," *Technics and Civilization*, (New York: Harcourt, Brace, & World, 1934), p.303-304.

Bernard Noel, *Magritte,* (New York: Crown Publishers, Inc., c. 1977), p.7.

Bernard Lavends, "Brownian Motion," *Scientific America,* February, 1985, vol. 252, p.81.

James Agee, *A Death in the Family*, (New York: McDowell, Obolensky, 1957), p.4.

Loren Eisely, "Charles Darwin," *Scientic America*, February, 1956, Vol.194, p. 70.

William Shakespeare, "Macbeth," *William Shakespeare: The Complete Works*, (New York: The Viking Press, 1971), Act v, scene v, p. 1133.

NOTES Continued

PART I GIVING PAUSE Continued

Franz Kafka, *Letter to His Father*, (New York: Schoken Press, 1974), pp.2526.

Gwendolyn Brooks, *A Report From Part One*, (Detroit: Broadside Press, 1973), p.44.

James Walcott, "Washington and the Gang of Five," *Vanity Fair*, November, 1984, p. 94.

Kenneth Gergen, "Multiple Identity," *Psychology Today* Magazine, May 1972, p.31.

Roger Neal, "From Rags to RAMS," *Forbes Magazine*, December 17, 1984, p.78.

Pauline Kael, "The Current Cinema," *The New Yorker*, October 1, 1984, p.111.

Dorothy Parker, "Mrs. Post Enlarges on Etiquette," *The Portable Dorothy Parker*, (New York: The Viking Press, 1980), p.476.

Philip Roth, "Conversion of the Jews," *Goodbye Columbus and Five Short Stories*, (New York: Modern Library/ Random House, 1966), pp.148, 150.

Katherine Anne Porter, "The Necessary Enemy," *The Collected Essays and Occasional Writing of Katherine Anne Porter*, (New York: Delacourte, 1970), p.74.

Jessica Mitford, *The American Way of Death*, (New York: Simon & Schuster, 1963), p.74.

E.E. Cummings, *i: Six Nonlectures IX*, (Cambridge: Harvard University Press, 1971), p. 2.

Ruth Bebe Hill, "Idiomatic Phrases," *Hanta Yo*, (New York: Doubleday & Co. Inc., 1979), pp.813-821.

Ralph Ellison, *The Invisible Man*, (New York: Signet Books, c.1952), p.7.

Germaine Greer, "The Stereotype," *The Female Eunuch*, (New York: McGraw-Hill, 1971), p.53.

Woody Allen, "Examining Psychic Phenomena," *The New Yorker*, October 7, 1972, pp. 32-33.

Alan Watt, "Murder in the Kitchen," *Does It Matter?*, (New York: Pantheon Books, 1970), p. 25-26.

Vladmir Nabokov, *Speak, Memory*, (New York: G.P.Putnam's Sons, 1966), p.19.

Jaclyn Fierman, "Beechnut Bounces Back," *Fortune Magazine*, December 24, 1984, Vol. 110, p.56.

Andy Rooney, "An Essay on War," *Literary Calvacade*, April 24, p. 38.

FINE-TUNING REALITY

"America's Top 100 Young Scientists," (ed. comment by Oliver Moore), *Science Digest*, December, 1984, Vol. 92, pp. 36-71.

Garry Trudeau, "Doonesberry," Universal Press Syndication, during weeks of 1982.

NOTES Continued

PART I SMOOTHING THE FLOW Continued

Richard Hall and Friends, *Sniglets: Any Word That Doesn't Appear in the Dictionary but Should*, (New York: Macmillan, 1984).

Elvis Presley, "Hound Dog," RCA Victor, July 1956. Words and music by Jerry Leiber and Mike Stoller.

Suzanne Muchnic, "Rowlandson's Best Is Laughable," *The Los Angeles Times*, January 5, 1985, Part V, p.6.

Octavio Paz, *Labyrinth of Sorrow*, (New York: Grove Press, 1961), p.37.

John Steinbech, "The Chrysanthemums," *The Long Valley*, (New York: Viking Press, 1973), p.9.

James Walcott, "Washington Talk and the Gang of Five," *Vanity Fair*, November 1984, p.94.

William Blake, "The Marriage Between Heaven & Hell," *Selected Poetry & Prose of William Blake*, ed. Northrop Frye, (Random House/ Modern Library, 1953), p.126.

Jim Murray, "Football Announcers — What They Say, What It Really Means," *The Los Angeles Times*, January 6, 1985, Part III, p.1.

Kay Larson, "Revolution by the Book," *New York Magazine*, December 3, 1984, p. 147.

Judges, 14:18, *The Bible*, Revised Standard Version.

Flannery O'Conner, "The Enduring Chill," *Everything That Rises Must Converge*, (New York: Farrar, Straus & Giroux, 1977), p.94.

Mark Twain, *The Adventures of Hucklebury Finn*, (Great Britain: Penquin Books, Ltd., 1979), p. 89.

Lewis Thomas, "The Lives of a Cell," *The Lives of a Cell: Notes of a Biology Watcher*, (New York: Viking Press, 1974), p.5.

Henry David Thoreau, *The Variorum Walden*, (New York: Washington Square Press, 1966), p.4.

J. Ellis and J. Norman, "How Tenesco Could Cash in on Harvester's Ills," *Businessweek*, December 3, 1984, p.31.

William Gass, *Habitations of the Word*, (New York: Simon & Schuster, 1985), p. 213.

MAKING FACES

Jim Murray, "Saying It Like It Is," *The Los Angeles Times*, December 2, 1979, Part III, p. 1, 20.

J. Robertson and G. Osbourne, "Postal System Input Buffer Device," *Datamation Magazine*. Date and page number NA.

anon., "Sytematic Buzz Phrase Projector," probably from Royal Canadian Air Force, popularized by Philip Broughton, U.S. Public Health Service Official.

NOTES Continued

PART I Continued
I am indebted to Shirley Sykes of San Diego Mesa College for the idea of this work out. See Shirley Sykes, "Gobbledygook in the Classroom," *inside english*, March 1983, p.3. In this article, Shirley recommends seeing good gobbledygooked examples of common expressions, famous quotation, and adages in Richard Altick's *Preface to Critical Reading*, 5th ed. (New York: Holt, Rinehart, & Winston, 1969), pp. 113-114.

PART II

RAISING THE DEAD
Fyodor Dostoyevsky, "The Grand Inquisitor," *The Brothers Karamozov*, trans. Constance Garnett, (New York, c.1950), Book V, p. 292-309.

SPLITTING THE SECOND
Natachee Scott Momaday, *House Made of Dawn*, (New York: Perennial Library, 1977), p. 20-21.

MOCKING WITH MASS MEDIA
Anthony Towne, "God Is Dead In Georgia," Excerpts from the Diaries of the Late God, *motive* magazine, (c) 1966 by the General Board of Higher Education and Ministry of the United Methodist Church. Reprinted with permission.

ANIMAL TALK
Roger Tory Peterson, "Greater Roadrunner," *A Field Guide to the Birds*, (Boston: Houghton Mifflin Co., 1980), p.182.

George E. Hollister, "With Legs Like These Who Needs Wings?," *National Wildlife* magazine, August, 1973, Vol. 11, pp. 12-13.

J.B.S. Haldane, "On Being the Right Size," *Possible Worlds and Other Papers*, (Freeport: Books for Libraries Press, 1971), pp. 20-28.

NICE GIANTS
Jim Murray, "Bubba — He's Just About the Biggest Pussycat Ever," *The Los Angeles Times*, March 10, 1985, Section III, p.1, 10.

Jim Murray, "These Guys Are Double and Trouble," *The Los Angeles Times*, March 1, 1985, Section III, p.1, 13.

Norman Mailer, "A Novel Biography," *Marilyn Monroe*, (New York: Grosset & Dunlap, 1973), pp.15-23.

UGLY GIANTS
Jonathan Swift, "A Voyage to Brobdingnag," *Gulliver's Travels*, (Great Britain: Penquin Books Ltd., 1979), pp.119-191.

Germaine Greer, "The Stereotype," *The Female Eunuch*, (New York: McGrawHill, 1971), pp. 47-55.

NOTES Continued

PART II Continued
THIRTEEN WAYS OF LOOKING AT A BLACKBIRD
Wallace Stevens, "Thirteen Ways of Looking at a Blackbird," *The Collected Poems of Wallace Stevens*, (New York: Alfred Knopf, 1954), pp. 92-95. (c.) 1954 by Wallace Stevens. Excerpts reprinted with permission of Alfred A. Knopf, Inc.

Kenneth Koch, *Rose, Where Did You Get That Red?*, (New York: Vintage Books, 1974), pp. 116-118.

E.H. Gombrich, "Art for Eternity," *The Story of Art*, (Great Britain: Phaidon Press, Ltd., 1968), pp. 35-41.

Peter Blauner, comp., "New York Style," *New York* magazine, December 24-31, 1984. Copyright (c) 1985 by News Group Publications, Inc. Excerpts reprinted with permission of *New York* magazine.

SLICED PIE
Erich Fromm, "Malignant Aggression: Necrophilia," *The Anatomy of Human Destructiveness*, (Holt, Rinehart, & Winston, 1973), pp. 325-367.

Jorge Luis Borges, "The Analytical Language of John Wilkins," *Other Inquisitions*, (Austin: University of Texas Press, 1964), p. 103.

Katherine Kuh, *Break-Up: The Core of Modern Art*, (Greenwich: New York Graphic Society, 1966), pp. 11-15.

Arnold J. Mandell, "Psychiatric Study of Professional Football," *Saturday Review World*, October 5, 1974, Vol. 2, pp. 12-16.

STRIP TEASE
Raymond Carver, "Will You Please Be Quiet, Please?," *Will You Please Be Quiet, Please?*, (New York: McGraw-Hill, 1976), pp.225-249.

Marvin Kaye, "The Toy With One Moving Part," *A Toy is Born*, (New York: Stein & Day, 1973), pp.71-79.

FLASHBACK
Delmore Schwartz, "In Dreams Begin Responsibility," *The World Is a Wedding*, (New York: New Directions, 1978).

George Kennan, "Flashbacks," *The New Yorker*, February 25, 1985, pp.52-69.

DOUBLE EXPOSURES
Erwin Knoll and Theodore Postol, "The Day the Bomb Went Off; an Imaginary Event," *The Progressive*, October, 1978, Vol. 42, pp.16-21.

Gwenda Blair, "Boobs in Toyland," *Village Voice*, May 11, 1982, pp. 20, 22.

DEVIL'S ADVICE
Mark Twain, "Advice to Youth," *Complete Essays of Mark Twain*, (New York: Doubleday, 1963), pp. 564-566.

Jonathan Swift, "A Modest Proposal," *The Norton Anthology of English Literature*, ed. M. H. Adams, (New York: W.W. Norton & Co., 1962), pp. 1389-1397.

William Blake, "The Marriage Between Heaven and Hell," *The Selected Poetry & Prose of William Blake, ed. Northrop Frye*, (New York: Random House/ Modern Library, 1953), pp. 122-134.

NOTES Continued

PART II Continued

TALKING WORDS

Jack Smith, "Time on his hands, love in his heart and Webster's Dictionary on his mind," *The Los Angeles Times,* March 3, 1985, Section IX, p.1.

anon., "The Talk of the Town: 'The Mystifier'," *The New Yorker,* March 4, 1985, pp. 35-36.

Jim Murray, "You Don't Punish a Guy Who's Fighting a Crime," *The Los Angeles Times,* June 28, 1983, Section III, p. 1, 7.

Ambrose Bierce, *The Enlarged Devil's Dictionary,* ed. Ernest Jerome Hopkins, (New York: Doubleday & Co., 1967).

Francis Bacon, "Of Suspicion," *Selected Writings of Francis Bacon,* (New York: Random House/ Modern Library, 1955), p.86.

Jack Smith, "On the scent of that most elusive of illusions — defining time, once and for all ... " *The Los Angeles Times,* March 11, 1985, Part V, p.1.

BLOOD FLOW

Erich Auerbach, "Odysseus' Scar," *Mimesis: The Representation of Reality in Western Literature,* (Princeton: Princeton University Press, 1968), pp. 3-23.

Barbara Tuchman, "This is the End of the World: The Black Death", *Distant Mirror: The Calamitous 14th Century,* (New York: Alfred A. Knopf, 1978), pp.92-125.

John Gliedman and William Roth, "Handicap as a Social Construction," *The Unexpected Minority,* For the Carnegie Council on Children, (New York: Harcourt, Brace, Jovanovich, 1980), pp.13-30.

Charles Darwin, "Worms and the Soil," *The Formation of Vegetable Mould, Through the Action of Worms, with Observations on Their Habits,* (New York: AMS Press, 1972).

DOORS

anon. "TRB from Washington: Handgun Mayhem," *The New Republic,* April 21, 1982, p. 4.

anon. "Harper's Index," *Harper's Magazine,* May, 1984, p.9. Statistics accurate as of March 14, 1984.

Tillie Olson, "Silences: When Writer's Don't Write," *Harper's Magazine,* October 1965, Vol. 231, pp. 153-156.

Bruno Bettelheim, *Freud and Man's Soul,* (New York: Alfred A. Knopf, 1982), Chapter 3, pp. 10-15.

Russell Baker, "Little Red Riding Hood Revisited," *New York Times,* January 13, 1980, p. 12.

Eric Berne, "Human Destiny," *What Do You Say After You Say Hello?,* (New York: Bantam Books, 1973), pp. 43-47.

Bruno Bettelheim, "Joey: A 'Mechanical Boy'," *Scientific America,* March, 1959 Vol. 200, pp. 34, 116-120 and May, p. 14^s.

Edward Hoagland, "The Courage of Turtles," *The Courage of Turtles:* fifteen essays about compassion, pain, and love ... (New York: Random House, 1970), pp. 20-30.

NOTES Continued

PART II   DOORS Continued

P.J. O'Rourke, "Foreigners Around the World," *National Lampoon,* May, 1976, pp. 73-77, 94, 97, 98, 100-103.

H.L.Mencken, "Le Contrat Social," *Prejudices: Third Series,* (New York: Octagon Books/ Farrar, Straus, & Giroux, 1977), pp. 289-292.

H.L.Mencken, "The Lure of Beauty," *A Mencken Chresomathy,* (New York: Alfred A. Knopf, 1953), pp. 36-39.

SQUEEZE PLAY

Gregory Corso, "Last Night I Drove a Car," *Gasoline,* copyright (c) 1955 by Gregory Corso, reprinted by permission of City Lights Books.

Andrew Marvel, "To His Coy Mistress," *The Norton Anthology of English Literature,* (New York: W.W.Norton & Co., Inc., 1962), p.868.

Sylvia Plath, "Daddy," *Aerial,* (New York: Harper & Row, 1965), p.49.

FINGER POINT

Thomas Jefferson and others, "The Declaration of Independence," *The Political Writings of Thomas Jefferson,* ed. Edward Dumbauld, (New York: Bobbs-Merrill Co., 1955), pp. 3-7.

David Sherwood, "Take My Wife — prithee," *American Heritage* magazine, April-May, 1984, Vol. 35, pp. 81-83.

Matthew, 5:1-7:28, *The Bible,* Revised Standard Version.

Lewis Thomas, "The Art of Teaching Science," *New York Times,* Section VI, March 14, 1982, p.89.

W.S. Merwin, "Unchopping a Tree," *The Miner's Pale Children,* (New York: Atheneum, 1970), pp. 85-88.

SINCERELY YOURS

Samuel Richardson, *Pamela,* (New York: Century, 1966).

Samuel Richardson, *Clarissa Harlowe,* (New York: Dutton, 1962).

Franz Kafka, *Letter to His Father,* (New York: Schocken Books, 1974).

Tobias Smollett, *Humphry Clinker,* (New York: Signet Classic, New American Library, c.1960), p.304-305.

Saul Bellow, *Herzog,* (New York: The Viking Press, 1967).

MASKS

J.D. Salinger, *The Catcher in the Rye,* (New York: Bantam Books, 1968), p.1.

The Editors, comp., "I Wish I'd Been There," *American Heritage,* December 1984, pp. 25-40.

NAY, IT IS. I KNOW NOT 'SEEMS.'

William Shakespeare, "The Tragedy of Prince Hamlet," *The Complete Works of William Shakespeare,* (New York: Viking/Penquin, 1969), Act I, sc. ii, pp. 936.

Edward T. Hall, "The Anthropology of Manners," *Scientific America,* April 1955, Vol. 192, pp. 20-21, 84-88.

NOTES Continued

PART II NAY, IT IS. I KNOW NOT 'SEEMS' Continued

X.J. Kennedy, "Who Killed King Kong," *Dissent*, Spring 1960, Vol.7, pp.213-215.

Garrett Mattingly, "Curtain Raiser," *The Armada*, (Boston: Houghton Mifflin, 1959), pp.1-6.

REAL MAGIC

Chris Van Allsburg, *Jumanji*, (Boston: Houghton Mifflin Co., c.1981).

Anais Nin, "January, 1936," *The Diaries of Anais Nin, Vol. 2, 1934-39*, (New York: The Swallow Press and Harcourt, Brace, and World, 1967), pp. 7181.

Anais Nin, "Summer, 1973," *The Diaries of Anais Nin, Vol. 7, 1966-1974*, (New York: Harcourt, Brace, Jovanovich, 1980), pp. 271-274.

Gabriel Garcia Marquez, *One Hundred Years of Solitude*, trans. Gregory Rabassa, (New York: Avon Books, 1973), pp. 137, 218-220.

John Updike, "Living Death," *The New Yorker*, May 20, 1985, p.118. Updike mentions Garcia Marquez's use of the term "brick-faced" in an interview by Peter Stone for *The Paris Review* in 1981.

Lewis Carroll, *Alice's Adventures in Wonderland*, (New York: Random House, special edition with the John Tenniel illustrations, 1946).

FRAME UPS

Plato, *The New Republic*, Book VII, trans. B. Jowett, (New York: Doubleday, 1960), pp. 205-209.

James Boswell, *The Life of Samuel Johnson*, (New York: Random House/ Modern library, 1952), pp. 123, 126, 306.

Art Buchwald, *...And Then I Told the President: The Secret Papers of Art Buchwald*, (New York: G.P. Putnam, 1965).

DUST IN THE LIBRARY

Roberta and Peter Markman, *10 Steps to Writing the Research Paper*, (Woodbury: Barron's Educational Series, 1982).

Joseph Gibalki and Walter S. Achstert, *MLA Handbook for Writers*, (New York: Modern Language Association). See latest edition.

Geoffrey Bibby, "The Body in the Bog," *Horizon*, (Winter, 1968), Vol. 10, pp. 44-51.

H.L. Menken, "A Neglected Anniversary (The Bathtub Hoax)," *The Bathtub Hoax & Other Blasts and Bravos*, (New York: Alfred A. Knopf, 1958), pp.410.

Jorge Luis Borges, *Labyrinths*, (New York: New Directions Publishing Corp., 1964).

BILLY FAULKNER

Elizabeth Mehren, "Lost Creativity Turns into Psychologist's Life Study," *The Los Angeles Times*, July 31, Section V, pp. 7-8. Also see Teresa Amabile's *The Social Pyschology of Creativity* (Springer/Verlag, 1983).

SUGGESTIONS:

Verve Press and the author of WRITEFUL are interested in your comments and suggestions regarding this book. They would especially enjoy having outstanding responses to the second and third work out option of the last chapter, "Billy Faulkner," for consideration as possible additions to future editions of WRITEFUL. Please include your name and address so you may be contacted in the eventuality that the author wishes to use your idea.

ADDITIONAL COPIES:

You may order additional copies of WRITEFUL by mail. For each copy of WRITEFUL send $8.95 plus $1.00 for shipping. If you cannot wait 3-4 weeks for book-rate shipping, send $2.50 for air shipping. California residents must also include 6% sales tax. (For example, California sales tax on one copy of WRITEFUL would be $ .54) Make check or money order out to Verve Press. Be sure to include your shipping address.

Send suggestions and book orders to:

Verve Press P.O. Box 1997 Huntington Beach, California, 92647.

PN 145 .H46

DATE DUE			
OCT 20 1991			